D1591233

MAKERS
of the
MUSLIM
WORLD

Chinggis Khan

SELECTION OF TITLES IN THE MAKERS OF
THE MUSLIM WORLD SERIES

Series editor: Patricia Crone,
Institute for Advanced Study, Princeton

'Abd al-Malik, Chase F. Robinson
Abd al-Rahman III, Maribel Fierro
Abu Nuwas, Philip Kennedy
Ahmad ibn Hanbal, Christopher Melchert
Ahmad Riza Khan Barelwi, Usha Sanyal
Al-Ma'mun, Michael Cooperson
Al-Mutanabbi, Margaret Larkin
Amir Khusraw, Sunil Sharma
El Hajj Beshir Agha, Jane Hathaway
Fazlallah Astarabadi and the Hurufis, Shazad Bashir
Ibn 'Arabi, William C. Chittick
Ibn Fudi, Ahmad Dallal
Ikhwan al-Safa, Godefroid de Callatay
Shaykh Mufid, Tamima Bayhom-Daou

For current information and details of other books in the
series, please visit www.oneworld-publications.com

MAKERS
of the
MUSLIM
WORLD

Chinggis Khan

MICHAL BIRAN

The Hebrew University of Jerusalem

ONEWORLD

OXFORD

CHINGGIS KHAN

A Oneworld Book
Published by Oneworld Publications 2007

ISBN-13: 978–1–85168–502–8

Typeset by Jayvee, Trivandrum, India
Printed and bound in India for Imprint Digital

Oneworld Publications
185 Banbury Road
Oxford OX2 7AR
England
www.oneworld-publications.com

CONTENTS

LIST OF MAPS, FIGURES AND ILLUSTRATIONS

MAPS

FIGURES

ILLUSTRATIONS

ACKNOWLEDGMENTS

I would first like to thank Patricia Crone, both for asking me to write this book and for her sharp editorial comments. My biggest debt is to my *quriltai* of experts, comprised of Tom Allsen, Reuven Amitai and David Morgan. Each of them read through the whole text and enriched it with many valuable comments, suggestions, and more idiomatic English, thereby greatly contributing to the book's final shape. I am also indebted to my colleague and friend Yuri Pines, my student Shay Shir, and my father Uzi Pumpian, who read the entire manuscript in the role of mythical general readers. Thanks are also due to Samuel N. Eisenstadt, Anatoly M. Khazanov and Ron Sela who commented on various chapters.

Many people helped me by suggesting, gathering and processing references. They include, apart from most of the above-mentioned, Manduhai Buyandelgeriyn, Yoav Di Kapua, Roy Fischel, Vincent Fourniau, Andrei Gomulin, Ziv Halevi, Sophia Katz, Fumihiko Kobayashi, Nimrod Luz, Timothy May, Hyunhee Park, Yael Sheinfeld, Gideon Shelach and Anke von Kugelagen. I am especially grateful to Maria Ivanics, who allowed me to use her translation of the *Daftar Chingiz namah* prior to its publication, and to Eyal Ginio for his expert and patient help with Ottoman texts. I also thank Tammar Sopher for producing the maps; Zeev Stossel for technical help; and the Metropolitan Museum for their permission to reproduce an illustration of Chinggis dividing his empire among his sons from a sixteenth-century Moghul manuscript of Rashid al-Din's *Jami' al-tawarikh* [1948 (48.144)]. Thanks go also to the students in my Mongol and Central Asian seminars at the Hebrew University.

All my friends suffered from my obsession with Chinggis Khan, but I would like to especially thank Nurit Stadler who sacrificed many coffee-breaks for discussing points, arcane and otherwise, in the Great Khan's biography. Lastly, I am also indebted to my sons, Yotam and Itamar, who already know about Chinggis Khan much more than is healthy for children of their age.

This book was supported by the Israel Science Foundation (grant no. 818/03).

INTRODUCTION: WHY CHINGGIS?

What event or occurrence has been more notable than the beginning of the
rule of Chinggis Khan, that it should be considered a new era?

Rashid al-Din [d. 1318], ed. Karīmī 1959: 1:16,
cited in Morgan 1988: 51

Chinggis Khan was not a Muslim. Why, then, should he be included in a
series entitled the *Makers of the Muslim World*?

The answer is simple: Chinggis Khan is included in this series because
he and his heirs made a real difference in the history of the Islamic world,
as the above quotation from the greatest historian of the Mongol era
clearly suggests. What is less obvious is the nature of this difference. On
the one hand, Chinggis Khan slaughtered many believers, pillaged their
riches and inflicted upon them an unprecedented disaster, so that he
came to be seen as the arch-enemy of Islam. On top of this, his grandson's
demolition of Baghdad is often seen as the end of medieval Islamic civilization, which thereafter lost its leading position in world history and
began to lag behind the West. This memory of the Mongol legacy is still
widespread, especially in the Arab world, and was recently invoked by
Saddam Hussein who, on the eve of the American invasion of Baghdad in
2003, depicted the U.S. government as the modern Mongols. In the
Turco-Iranian world, on the other hand, Chinggis Khan also became the
revered father of, and a source of political legitimacy for, several Muslim
dynasties, especially after the conversion to Islam of the Mongols in Iran
and, later, in southern Russia and Central Asia. Chinggis's descendants
ruled over significant parts of the Muslim world up to the eighteenth and
nineteenth centuries, and he was therefore given a place in the pantheon
of Muslim heroic figures. Thus Chinggis's biography became an integral
part of Muslim historiography, and the political and religious needs of

1

Chinggisid and even some non-Chinggisid rulers therefore influenced the way Chinggis Khan has come to be depicted in different Muslim contexts. Moreover, institutions and concepts of legitimation ascribed to the Great Khan were instrumental in shaping much of the late medieval and early modern world, in the Abode of Islam and beyond, and the intellectual horizons, political boundaries, and ethnic composition of the post-thirteenth-century Muslim world were deeply affected by Chinggisid rule. Chinggis Khan therefore was not only a destructive force in the Islamic world but also a constructive influence, whose legacy survived, especially in Central Asia, long after his death and well into the modern era.

This perspective is also the answer to another obvious question: why another book on Chinggis Khan? There is no dearth of books dedicated to the great conqueror, recently crowned by *The Washington Post* as the man of the (second) millennium, and several recent books provide a more positive and complex picture of him than in the past (e.g. Weatherford 2004; Lane 2004). Yet a book concentrating on his role in the Muslim world has not yet been written. Even those who stress Chinggis Khan's role in the shaping of the modern world emphasize the connections between Europe and China, marginalizing his impact on the Muslim world. Moreover, unlike many other biographies of Chinggis Khan, this book, though written mainly for a general audience, is based on close reading in a vast array of primary sources from the Islamic world and beyond; it also incorporates the recent upsurge of new and innovative research on the Mongol Empire.

The volume starts with a short description of steppe society and the political situation in Asia and the world of Islam before the rise of Chinggis Khan. The second chapter reviews the society in which Temüjin, the future Chinggis Khan, was born and rose to prominence, tracing his career until he was enthroned as Chinggis Khan in the assembly (*quriltai*) of 1206. The third chapter analyses his conquests, with special emphasis on his invasion of the Muslim world and its implications, and tries to explain the factors behind the overwhelming success of these conquests. The fourth chapter summarizes the major effects of the Chinggisid enterprise on the Muslim world, stressing the persistence of Chinggis's descendants as rulers of Muslim states and their contribution to the broadening of the horizons of the Muslims and to the further expansion of the world of Islam. It also reviews the legacy of Mongol statecraft, emphasizing the role of Chinggisid institutions, especially concepts of legitimation and law in the Turco-Iranian world, as well as the Mongol impact on ethnic and geopolitical changes in the Muslim world. The fifth chapter discusses the different images of Chinggis Khan in various Muslim contexts. It looks at how Chinggis's new role as a founding father of Muslim dynasties, and originator of the political and social order for which they stood, required a reshaping of his biography in different Muslim contexts in the centuries following his death, and how the rise of nationalism marginalized his role in Muslim history and brought him back into the position of an accursed enemy. The last chapter compares Chinggis's position in the Muslim world with the evolution of his myth in other contexts, mainly in Mongolia and China but also in Russia and the West, thereby providing a comparative approach in which to view Chinggis's afterlife in the Muslim world.

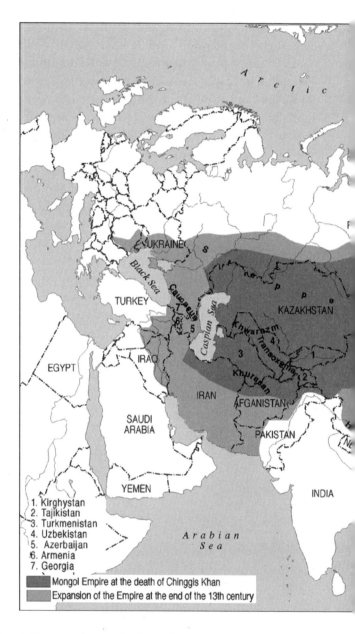

Map 1. The Mongol Empire by the Death of Chinggis Khan and in the Height of its Expansion

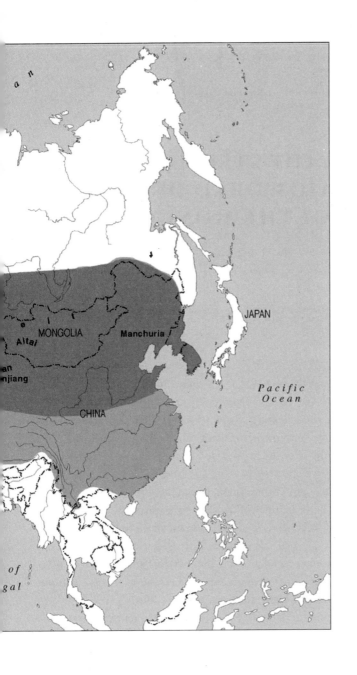

ASIA, THE STEPPE, AND THE ISLAMIC WORLD ON THE EVE OF THE MONGOLS

The Tatars are from the Turkic people, and the Turks are all from the offspring of Kumar b. Japheth

Ibn Khaldun [d.1406] 1957: 5:1098

Chinggis Khan set the stage for a new phase in Muslim and world history, yet he was a successor to many centuries of interaction between the nomads and the sedentary world. Chinggis Khan's hordes were not the first to advance into the Islamic world from the region known after them as Mongolia. They were preceded by the Turks, who ruled a vast region stretching from Manchuria to the Caspian sea in the sixth and seventh centuries, and Muslim Turks, descendants of the subjects of the Turkic empire, ruled in much of the eastern Islamic world on the eve of Chinggis Khan's accession. The Turkic advance into the Muslim world was much more gradual – and much less traumatic – than that of the Mongols, yet their precedent, and the fact that most of them were Muslims by the time the Mongols appeared on the scene, had a lasting effect on the Mongols' later relations with the Muslim world. In fact, due to their common nomadic lifestyle, the Mongols were often conceived of by Muslim writers as a new kind of Turk.

The Mongols can be seen as the continuators of two Turkic traditions. First, the legacy of the steppe empires established in Mongolia, among which the Turkic empire was by far the most important, and second, the legacy of the Mongols' immediate predecessors, the nomadic (or semi-nomadic) inter-regional states that arose in Manchuria and Central Asia in the tenth to twelfth centuries; the Central Asian ones were mainly founded by Muslim Turks. This chapter reviews these two legacies and the continuities between the Mongols and their predecessors; yet, before doing so, it begins with a short overview of steppe nomadism as practiced by Chinggis Khan and his precursors. In order to complete the background to the pre-Chinggisid world, the chapter then introduces the major political entities in Asia on the eve of Chinggis's appearance and concludes with the ways they shaped his rise to power.

STEPPE NOMADISM

Mongolia is part of the Eurasian steppe belt which stretches from Manchuria in north-eastern China to Hungary in Eastern Europe, bounded by the Taiga forests in the north and by a desert belt in the south. Although mountain ranges rise in the steppe margins, the steppe is basically a flat, treeless plateau, without significant barriers which would restrict movement. The largest land empires ever created – the Turkic, the Mongol, and the Russian – ruled in this realm. Ecologically, the steppe belt is a continental, northern and arid region, characterized by marginal rainfall, short growing seasons and a harsh climate, with tremendous differences between day and night, summer and winter. This unforgiving environment supports very low population densities: the Republic of Mongolia, Chinggis Khan's homeland, also known as Outer Mongolia[1], is larger than France, Germany, the United Kingdom and Italy combined; its population, however, numbers only about 2.5 million people. The wealth of a Mongol chief was therefore mainly measured in people (and livestock), not in territory.

[1] Outer Mongolia as opposed to Inner Mongolia, also part of Chinggis's homeland, which is now a Chinese province bordering the republic of Mongolia. The division originated in the seventeenth century when the Mongols, first the Inner or more southern confederations and then the Outer, or northerners, submitted to the Manchus, who ruled China from 1644 to 1911. See chapter six.

The steppe environment supports only marginal agriculture, mainly in river valleys, yet the limited rainfall (250–500 ml a year) produces rich grassland, which provides good pastures, making pastoral nomadism the main source of subsistence throughout the steppe. Most of the needs of the pastoralists – herdsmen of goats, cattle, camels and above all of sheep and horses – are provided by their livestock. These mainly include meat and milk products (including *qumis*, the alcoholic beverage derived from fermented mare's milk, the steppe's beer), wool (used also to make felt for covering tents), and hides. To provide the best possible grazing grounds for their mixed herds, most of the herding population moves seasonally "in search of water and grass". This movement, however, is not haphazard or aimless, but follows an annual, and usually fixed, cycle from summer to winter camps, sometimes with alternative spring and autumn camps as well. The migrations are not necessarily very long – an annual cycle of 150–600 km was common in Mongolia – yet calculating the migration's route and schedule, taking into account the needs of the mixed herds, requires careful planning, which the Mongols later put to use in their military campaigns.

Even when expertly planned, however, the nomadic economy is fragile and hardly autarkic. The livestock wealth of the nomads is vulnerable to adverse weather conditions and disease, and unlike farmers, nomads cannot amass their beasts for a rainy (or all too dry) day. Nor can a pastoral economy supply grains, raw materials or many manufactured goods: a pure nomad is a poor nomad. The nomads usually supplemented their pastoral economy with hunting, which also provided military training and entertainment, and even with marginal agriculture in the river valleys. Yet to have a more convenient existence, they depended on their sedentary neighbors.

Sedentary supplies can be acquired in several ways, such as by trade, diplomacy, raids or conquest. Since pastoral nomadism has certain characteristics – mainly mobility – which lend themselves to successful war, the nomads usually secured their relationship with the sedentary population through the tremendous military advantage they had – until the modern period – over most of their sedentary neighbors. Nomadic life requires every man – and woman – to ride and shoot from an early age, to develop survival skills and resilience and to adapt constantly to changing circumstances. Moreover, everyday missions, such as supervising the herds or participating in hunting, served as military training too, for both individuals and groups. There is no word for soldier in Mongolian, since every nomad became a soldier through coping with the steppe's daily challenges.

The main social unit in the steppe was the tribe. The tribe was based on shared political and economic interests and centered around its chief, although most of its members were also connected by – real or (mostly) spurious – genealogical ties to one putative ancestor. As a political unit, roughly whatever following a chief could muster, the tribe could be ethnically and linguistically heterogeneous. Many of the Mongol tribes in Chinggis's time contained both Turkic and Mongol elements and the *Secret History*, the main Mongol source for Chinggis's reign, defines them as people of nine tongues.

The tribe was a rather fluid structure, mainly due to the lack of an orderly succession system in the steppe. Two contradictory succession modes coexisted – lineal and lateral. According to the lineal tradition, succession passed from father to son; according to the lateral mode, succession passed to the chiefly clan's senior male, usually the late chief's brother, moving down to the youngest brother before passing to the next generation. This meant that with each chief's demise there were several competing candidates, whom other members of the leading clan would often join. The choice among them was usually based on talent: the most competent of the eligible heirs was elected to succeed. The election of a new chief was confirmed in several rites, and in the Mongol case it was solemnly declared in a grand assembly (*quriltai*) of the tribal nobility. Yet succession struggles were part and parcel of tribal politics, and the losers often tended to split off and create their own units.

Another reason for the fluidity of the tribal system was the tribe's complex structure. The tribe was constructed of a varying number of hypothetically related clans and lineages, each containing several (roughly five to 100) families. Lineages could easily split, as a result of internal discord or an increase in numbers, and divide into several branch lineages, not all of them necessarily remaining with the original tribe. Alternatively, they could incorporate other lineages and grow to become a clan or even a rival tribe to their original unit.

Besides the division into descent groups, the tribe was also separated into several strata: nobles, commoners and dependencies. The nobles, known as white heads or bones, owed their status to their direct descent from the tribe's or lineage's progenitor, and provided the tribe's political leadership. The junior or collateral lines of the descent groups formed the commoners, known as the black heads or bones. Though the nobles usually had bigger herds and better pasturelands, there was no sharp social distinction between the two lines, nor was there any dramatic difference in lifestyle. At the bottom of the social ladder were the dependents or slaves, usually acquired in raids on nearby tribes or sedentary people. Devoid of their own herds, they were obliged to work for their masters as herders, domestics or agricultural laborers and to join them in battle.

Another component of the tribe, and a major device for founding alliances in non-kinship terms, were the *nökers* (companions). A *nöker* was an individual who chose to attach himself to a leader of his own choice despite the lack of any kinship between the two. Renouncing his blood loyalty to his own clan, the *nöker* provided military support or any other commission for his chosen lord, and in return received protection, provisions and food. *Nökers* were recruited from various social strata and origins and they were the main instrument through which a rising talented chief, such as Chinggis Khan, could acquire a following.

Tribes in Mongolia were exogamous, meaning that they married only outside the tribe, and marriage alliances were an important device for cementing inter-tribal coalitions. Polygamy was common, though there was a distinction between the principal wife and lesser women and only the sons of the former were eligible as successors for their father's positions. Women played an important role in all aspects of tribal life, including fighting, and sometimes enjoyed real political power: several Chinggisid *khatuns* (noble ladies) served as the empire's regents after their husbands' demise.

Another form of inter-tribal alliances was the *anda*, sworn or blood brother. This was a voluntary alliance between equals (often chiefs) who chose to treat each other as brothers. They strengthened their oath by drinking from a beaker in which a few drops of the new brothers' blood were mixed, and the alliance was considered more bonding than natural kinship.

Another channel of inter-tribal relations was the shaman, the Mongol "priest," the mediator between the nomads and the supernatural world. At the head of the supernatural hierarchy was the blue and eternal heaven (*köke möngke Tengri*), the sky god of the steppe, quite a natural choice in a treeless, seldom cloudy, landscape. Beneath Tengri (and his much less significant "wife," the earth and fertility goddess, Itügen), but above the world of men, was the world of the spirits, representing either human ancestors or physical phenomena such as trees, mountains, and winds. While in a trance, the shaman was able to move between the different worlds, connecting men to spirits and even having a direct link to Tengri. Dressed in white, the steppe's most honored color, carrying a drum and adorned with various kinds of insignia (often wolves' skin) to help him enter into a trance, the shaman performed different kinds of divination and healing. Consulted in all important occasions such as child birth, war, the planning of a journey, weather forecasts, and ceremonies, the shaman easily gathered considerable political power which he could use for or against his tribal chief. Moreover, as a member of the shamans' "guild," the shaman (or shamaness) would wander among different tribes, and the links he acquired often benefited his own tribe. The practice of shamanism did not prevent the nomads from adopting other religions – as in East Asia in general, religion was not exclusive in Mongolia. The nomads were familiar with many religions, and could adhere to several of them simultaneously. Even if they did not subscribe to them, however, the inclusive nature of religion usually resulted in tolerance toward all religions.

The tribal organization sufficed for most of the nomads' everyday needs, such as defining migration routes, solving conflicts and even arranging small-scale raids. However, the emergence of a supra-tribal unit, from confederation to more centralized nomadic empires, was not uncommon. The most complex and enduring nomadic empires arose in Mongolia, where the ecological boundary between steppe and town is the clearest and where the tribesmen were confronted with China, the greatest and most enduring sedentary empire in the region. The nomadic empires usually arose in times of crisis, often related to the necessity of coping with a sedentary neighbor. The creation of a supra-tribal unit was therefore basically ephemeral (like dictatorship in

Rome). Its maintenance was highly dependent on the personality of the empire's leader, and on his ability continuously to reward his followers, who, being nomads, could easily decamp for greener pastures. This reward was usually dependent on the leader's ability to extort goods from his sedentary neighbors, by either trade, diplomacy, raids or conquest. Gradually, nomadic empires also developed other means which helped them preserve their unity, means which were inherited by Chinggis's Mongols.

THE LEGACY OF THE STEPPE EMPIRES

In terms of political culture, religion and military organization, the Mongols followed the precedents of former steppe empires that originated in Mongolia, notably the Xiongnu (third century B.C.E. to fourth century C.E.), the Turks (sixth to eighth centuries), and their successors, the Uighurs (744–840), among which the Turkic Empire was by far the most influential. These empires developed an ideology that legitimated the emergence and maintenance of a supra-tribal structure, and employed a military organization that was a crucial element in the consolidation of such a structure.

The focus of the steppe ideology and the primary source of super-tribal unity in the steppe world was Tengri (Heaven), the supreme sky god of the steppe, who was able to confer the right to rule on earth on a single clan.[2] The heavenly charisma resided in the whole royal clan; each of his members could theoretically be elevated to the Khaqanate, the supreme office of the ruler, while non-members were not eligible candidates for the throne. The Khaqan was the political and military leader of the empire, and his possession of the mandate from Tengri was confirmed by success in battle on the one hand, and by shamanic ceremonies on the other. As Tengri did not bestow his mandate on every generation (i.e. the steppe world was often left without a unifying Khaqan), this confirmation

---

[2] Whether this notion originated in the Chinese concept of the Mandate of Heaven, in a similar Iranian concept or in an Indo-Aryan concept brought first to the steppe and then into China, is beside the point for our survey.

was important for securing the Khaqan's power. Yet the Khaqan also had certain shamanic functions of his own, which enabled him to dismiss shamans whenever they threatened his authority. The center of the world ruled by the Khaqan was the area around the Ötükän mountains near the Orkhon river in Central Mongolia, a territory that was already considered the sacred land of the nomadic world under the Xiongnu. It was there the Turks left the famous Orkhon inscriptions in the eighth century and where the Mongol capital, Qara Qorum, was built more than four hundred years later.

Apart from ideology, another long-lived feature of the steppe imperial tradition was decimal military organization, first attested under the Xiongnu. The army was organized in decimal units of 10, 100, 1000 and 10,000, and since every nomad was a soldier, the military organization was actually an important means of social organization. Although up to the time of Chinggis Khan the decimal units were arranged along roughly tribal lines, their existence was an important mechanism of control that enabled the Khaqan to bypass and neutralize tribal cohesion and authority. The decimal organization was also useful for incorporating new nomads into the empire's army. The establishment of a royal guard, also attested from the Xiongnu onward, served the same functions and enabled the ruler to create a new elite, personally loyal to him, thereby also contributing to the longevity of the empire.

Decimal organization and Turkic ideology were used also by the imperial successors to the Turks, the Uighurs in Mongolia (744–840) and the Khazars in the European steppe (ca. 620s–965). Both ruled over empires of a smaller scale and in both the elite also adopted a universal religion, Manichaeism and Judaism respectively, side by side with its Turkic tradition. Even though no nomadic people aspired to unite the steppe from the collapse of those empires until the rise of the Mongols, its universal tradition still served as "an ideology in reserve" (Di Cosmo 1999: 20), ready to be revived if the creation of a supra-tribal empire were to be attempted again.

Despite the ideology of the Khaqan's world dominion and his disciplined army, and despite the vast territory controlled by the Turks at the height of their power – from the borders of China to the Byzantine frontiers – neither the Turks nor their pre-Chinggisid successors in Mongolia ever tried to conquer the sedentary states that bordered the steppe. Instead they consciously preferred to remain in the steppe, using their mobility and superior military skills to secure their economic interests in the sedentary world through raids, war and diplomacy, which enabled them to obtain tribute, trade, or revenues from China and other sedentary powers. The world which Tengri bestowed upon the Khaqan to rule was, until the rise of Chinggis Khan, the world of the steppe.

The Immediate Predecessors: The Inter-Regional States

The period that immediately preceded that of the Mongols did not witness the rise of a new steppe empire, but rather the emergence of another kind of state in the Steppe. Emerging from the tenth century onward, these states originated not in Mongolia but either in Manchuria or in Central Asia, that is, in regions in which nomad and sedentary coexistence was much more prevalent than in the Mongolian steppe. They rose to power against the background of a power vacuum that had characterized the steppe since the fall of the Uighurs (840) and the decline of the sedentary empires that bordered the steppe: the collapse of Tang China (906), the fragmentation of the Abbasid Caliphate (based in Baghdad) from the middle of the ninth century, and the decline of the Samanids in north-eastern Iran and Transoxania from the mid tenth century. In the western steppes, these states were established by splinter groups of the Turks, such as the Qarakhanids (c. 950–1213) and the Seljuqs (c. 1044–1194), or former mamluks (military slaves) such as the Khwarazm Shahs (c. 1097–1231); while in the east, and of more immediate relevance for the Mongols, the founders were Manchurian peoples. The first were the Khitans, once part of the Turkic world, under significant Uighur influence, who established the Liao dynasty (907–1125) and later the Qara Khitai (Western Liao) dynasty in Central Asia (1124–1218). The Khitans' successors in northern China were the Jurchens, their former vassals, who founded the Jin dynasty (1115–1234).

Unlike their steppe predecessors, these peoples did conquer parts of the sedentary states that bordered the steppe, thereby creating empires in which a nomadic (or semi-nomadic) minority, backed by a strong military machine, ruled over a multi-ethnic nomadic and sedentary population. This in turn required appropriate administrative skills as well as new forms of legitimation. In establishing these states, the rulers became closely associated with the sedentary traditions of the areas over parts of which they ruled, whether Chinese in the eastern steppe or Muslim in the western steppe (and in the case of Hungary, even Christian). This sedentary influence played an important role in the shaping of the royal institutions and the administrations of these states, which included direct taxation of the sedentary population side by side with tribute from China (in the eastern steppe) or a variety of indirect means of revenue collection (in the western steppe). Yet these outside influences did not eradicate the steppe past, which remained a major part of the elite identity and government, even after some of the rulers of these states became settled.

The pre-imperial history of the Mongols was closely associated with the Manchurian dynasties. It was only after the Liao Khitans conquered Manchuria in the early tenth century, driving most of its original Turkic population westward, that the ancestors of Chinggis Khan entered Mongolia. Coming from the region of the Liao river in southern Manchuria, the Liao ruled over Manchuria, Mongolia and a small part of northern China, centered around contemporary Beijing and known as the sixteen prefectures, the only part of China-proper that the contemporary and ethnically Chinese Song dynasty (960–1279) was unable to re-conquer during its attempt to unify the country. While the Chinese territory was a small part of the Khitan realm, it was by far the most populous and, economically, most important part of their empire. The Khitans used a dual administration to control their complex realm: the northern branch of the administration, mostly staffed by Khitans holding Khitan titles and wearing Khitan dress, controlled the affairs of the nomads, Khitans, Mongols and others who retained their tribal structure. The southern branch, staffed by Chinese and Khitans holding Chinese titles and wearing Chinese dress, handled the affairs of the mostly Chinese sedentary population by retaining the pre-conquest, Chinese bureaucracy.

Throughout their period of domination the Khitans remained preponderantly nomadic, and their emperor moved throughout the year among his seasonal camps and the five capitals of his kingdom, with his court following closely behind. Khitan cultural identity was also expressed in their national scripts, still only partially deciphered, and in their unique material culture, which is now well known through many recent excavations in China. Simultaneously, however, the Khitans adopted the Chinese imperial tradition and portrayed themselves, at home and abroad, as champions of Chinese culture, no less than the Song. Moreover, due to their military superiority, gained by their nomadic forces that had access to weaponry and equipment produced by the sedentary sector of their state, the Khitans managed to compel the Song dynasty not only to pay considerable annual tributes of silk and silver, but also to acknowledge them as equals. The Khitan emperor therefore bore the title of the northern Son of Heaven, equal in status to the Song emperor, the southern Son of Heaven, a division which stands in sharp contrast to the original Chinese concept of "one sun in the sky and one emperor upon earth." The money and goods extorted from the Song formed the basis for extensive Khitan commerce with lands to the west. It was in this way that the ethnonym Khitan, in its Turkic form Khitai (from which is derived Cathay in English), came to be associated with China in the Muslim world, Russia and Medieval Europe. By combining different traditions, the Khitans managed to rule China, albeit only a small part of it, without leaving "the back of the horse," i.e. without giving up their nomadic ways, thereby setting a certain precedent for the Mongols. Moreover, Liao garrisons and the cities they established in Mongolia earned the Khitans great prestige among the ancestors of Chinggis Khan. They also served as a channel for the transmission of Chinese and Khitan institutions, such as the system of the *jam* (postal relay system) and the *ordo* (camp of the ruler or a prince), to the Chinggisids.

In the early twelfth century, however, the declining power of the Liao emperors and their economic difficulties prompted the Jurchens, a north-Manchurian subject tribe, to rebel. In 1114 a full-scale war broke out between the Khitans and the Jurchens, resulting in the establishment of the Jurchen dynasty known as the Jin (1115–1234), which succeeded the Liao in 1125. The Jin not only subdued the Liao, but advanced further into northern China. In 1127 they took over most of the north, up to the

Huai river, pushing the Song dynasty (thereafter known as the Southern Song) hundreds of miles southward. The Jin retained the status of the Northern Son of Heaven and the right of extracting tribute from the Song. But the Jin were much closer to their far more numerous Chinese subjects than the Liao, who kept one foot on the steppe, and they soon abandoned Liao-style dual administration in favor of a Chinese-style bureaucracy, although they did successfully maintain their own identity. Unlike the Liao, the Jin never conquered Mongolia. Instead they skillfully implemented the old Chinese policy of "using barbarians to control barbarians," or divide and rule, supporting one tribe against another and then transferring their support whenever their original ally became too strong.

While most of the Liao Khitans surrendered to the Jin, one Khitan Prince, Yelü Dashi, preferred to move westward, hoping to return later to restore the Liao dynasty in its former domains. After six years in western Mongolia, Dashi recognized his inability to challenge the Jurchen Jin dynasty, and, aware of the relative weakness of the Central Asian kingdoms, he decided to seek a political future further to the west. In a little more than a decade he successfully fashioned a new empire in Central Asia that was known to the Muslims as the Qara Khitai (the Black Khitans) and to China as the Xi Liao (Western Liao). After completing their conquests in 1141, the Qara Khitai empire ruled the area stretching between the Oxus river in the west and the Altai mountains in the east, i.e., most of the modern Central Asian republics (Kirghizistan, Uzbekistan, Tajikistan and south Kazakhstan) as well as Xinjiang in present-day China, and at least until 1175 they also exercised a certain sovereignty over western Mongolia, especially the Naiman tribe. The Qara Khitai rulers bore the title Gürkan, universal khan, and were also designated as Chinese emperors. The Qara Khitai were Buddhists yet they ruled over a heterogeneous, multi-ethnic, but mostly Muslim, population. They used a unique blend of Chinese, Inner Asian and Muslim forms of government to achieve a period of relative prosperity and stability in Central Asia. Their empire was divided into a central territory, ruled directly from the Qara Khitai capital Balasaghun, in north Kirgizstan, and a cluster of subject kingdoms and tribes surrounding it, which were ruled indirectly.

Among the subject kingdoms, which included the eastern and western Qarakhanids described below, the Gaochang kingdom of the Uighurs deserves special mention, due to its later significance for the Mongols. This oasis state had been established by the remnants of the Uighur empire who migrated from Mongolia to the region of modern eastern Xinjiang (around Turfan) when the Kirgiz took over their empire in 840. It was based mainly on trade and gradually became Buddhist. The Uighurs acquired a reputation as cultural brokers, and their familiarity with both steppe traditions and sedentary life was highly appreciated by Chinggis Khan and his heirs. Under the Qara Khitai, the Uighur leader, called the Idiqut, had to acknowledge Qara Khitai supremacy and to comply with their initially modest financial and military demands. He was, however, able to preserve both his title and his army, as were most other Qara Khitai vassals, since the Khitans deliberately tried to minimize the change in their subjects' life.

The Mongols were aware of the Qara Khitai, and much of their trade with Muslim Central Asia seemed to have been conducted through Qara Khitai subjects. Moreover, the unique blend of Qara Khitai institutions was highly significant for the Mongols, since by using Chinese trappings to rule over a mostly Muslim population, the Qara Khitai narrowed the gap between the ways of ruling in Central Asia and in China, thereby facilitating Mongol ability to borrow traditions and personnel from both directions.

In the Muslim world, the equivalents of the Liao and Jin were the Turkic dynasties of the Qarakhanids and Seljuqs. While they did not have a direct impact on the Mongols, a few words about them, and about the role of the Turks in the Muslim world in general, are needed for understanding the pre-Mongol Muslim world. The Muslims first met the Turks in Central Asia in the eighth century when the latter's imperial heyday was already over, but they nonetheless soon learned to appreciate the Turks' military prowess. From the ninth century onward the Turks became an increasingly important factor in the Muslim armies, both under the Abbasid caliphs (750–1258) and in the regional dynasties that emerged from the ninth century onward as the caliphs' power declined. Most of the Turks entered into the abode of Islam as *mamluks* or *ghulams*, military slaves, bought as boys and trained to serve as elite soldiers in the Muslim armies. The Turks therefore first entered the

Muslim world as individuals, some of whom reached important posts and eventually established their own dynasties. From the tenth century onward they began to arrive as groups as, mainly under the influence of the Iranian Samanid dynasty which ruled from Bukhara (875–1005), Turkic tribes living outside the realm of the abode of Islam adopted Islam. They advanced into the Muslim world and soon began to rule parts of it. The first Turco-Muslim dynasty was the Qarakhanids, who embraced Islam in the region of Kashgar (today China's western-most city) and began to expand into the Muslim world. In 999 they conquered Transoxania from the Samanids, while the more western territories of the Samanids were taken by another Turkic-Muslim dynasty, the Ghaznavids (994–1186), who rose from the ranks of the Samanids' military slaves.

The Qarakhanid-Ghaznavid wars, together with a chain of migrations set in motion by the Khitans' subjugation of Mongolia in the tenth century and by the emergence of the Tangut state in 1032 (about which see below), brought about the rise of the Seljuq Turks. Originating in the Turkic Oghuz tribes and embracing Islam in the late tenth century. In 1040 the Seljuqs defeated the Ghaznavids in Dandānqān near Marw, and, continuing westward, they entered Baghdad in 1055, moving from the margins of the Islamic world into its center. There the Seljuqs overthrew the Iranian Buyid (also known as Buwayhid) dynasty (935–1055) and proclaimed themselves Sultans, becoming the real power behind the Abbasid Caliphs. Arriving as Sunni Muslim (as opposed to the Shiite Buyids) and following the gradual penetration of Turks into the Muslim world, the Seljuqs met with little opposition when they took over the heart of the Islamic world. In Baghdad they appointed themselves Sultans (literally: 'powers') and took over most of the practical aspects of rulership, thereby marginalizing the Caliph, who, however, remained the symbol of Islamic unity and provided legitimacy for the Seljuqs and for all the other Turkic dynasties. The Seljuqs' further success against the infidels – they defeated the Byzantine emperor in 1071, thereby laying Anatolia open to Turkish penetration – strengthened their fame as warriors for the faith. Soon after their achievements in the west, the Seljuqs renewed their interest in Central Asia. Meanwhile, from the mid eleventh century onward, the Qarakhanids were divided into a western khanate, centered in Transoxania, and an eastern khanate, which ruled in eastern Turkestan and Semirechye. In 1089 the Seljuqs took over Bukhara and Samarqand and made the Western Qarakhanids their vassals, and soon afterwards the Eastern Qarakhanids surrendered as well.

The Seljuq administration can be described as a dual administration preserving steppe and sawn traditions in a way which has some similarities with the Liao case. The central administration was divided into the *diwan* and the *dargah* (court). The *diwan* dealt with the civil management, mainly with the collection of taxes. Staffed with Persian bureaucracy and headed by the vizier, this wing of the administration continued the traditional Abbasid patterns of government. The *dargah* was mainly military in character, and also had judiciary authority. It was staffed mainly with Turkish military commanders and also with members of subject rulers' families kept as hostages. The court was itinerant and moved between the several capitals of the Seljuqs. Yet the Seljuqs did not remain nomadic, unlike the Khitans, and they experienced constant problems controlling the considerable nomadic Oghuz population, known as Turcoman, who continued to pour into the Middle East. The Seljuqs transferred most of these nomads to the frontiers, using their military skills in Anatolia and Azerbaijan, and established a strong and loyal Mamluk force to balance the tribal army, yet the Turcoman continued to threaten the stability of the state well into the twelfth century.

Most of the Seljuq empire was governed indirectly, by local dynasties who had ruled the areas before the arrival of the Seljuqs (e.g. the Caspian provinces; Qarakhanid Central Asia); by tribes that were allowed a considerable degree of autonomy (in Gurgan, Azerbaijan, Khuzistan and Iraq); or through the *iqta'* system. The *iqta',* an assignment of land or its revenue as a kind of salary, given mostly to military commanders, was an established Muslim method of payment, which, however, became much more widespread under the Seljuqs. The *iqta'* saved the central government the need to find cash to pay its troops and facilitated the control of the provinces. Originally the *iqta'* did not include governing functions, apart from the collection of taxes, and it was never meant to be hereditary, but as the power of the central government weakened, *iqta'* holders became more independent, thereby contributing to the disintegration of the empire. Another institution which reflects Seljuq steppe political culture and eventually also contributed to their fall was that of the *atabeg*. The *atabeg* (Turkic: 'father-prince') was a Turkic commander appointed to act as guardian and tutor to a young Seljuq prince, who had been given a city or province to rule on his behalf until he was of age. The relationship was often cemented by a marriage between the *atabeg* and the prince's mother. This system functioned properly when the central government was strong, but as it weakened, the *atabeg*s often deprived the princes of their authority and created their own dynasties.

Indeed, by the late eleventh century, following the death of Sultan Malikshah and his famous vizier Nizam al-Mulk, the Seljuqs also fell prey to family rivalries and internecine strife. These resulted in attempts by subject dynasties to assert their independence and in the rise of local dynasties, either from the ranks of the provincial governors and *iqta'* holders, or from the ranks of Seljuq *atabeg*s. Seljuq weakness was first apparent in the west, Iran and Iraq, because the east was still ruled from Khurasan by the great Seljuq sultan, Sanjar (1118–1157). Yet Sanjar's later years were full of challenges. In 1141 he suffered a major defeat at the hands of the Qara Khitai, who took over Transoxania. Their victory also gave rise to a massive Oghuz migration into Khurasan, where they threatened the very center of Seljuq rule, and even managed to hold Sanjar as a prisoner in a golden cage for a few years. Sanjar's weakness paved the way for the rise of a new power, one that not only eliminated the Seljuqs, but was also the first Muslim power that later had to confront the Mongols – the Khwarazm Shahs.

Centered along the lower course and delta of the Oxus, in the north of modern Uzbekistan, Khwarazm sometimes brought the neighboring steppe and desert areas under its political and cultural influence. Even though it was connected by caravan routes to the Volga, Bukhara and northern Iran, it was nonetheless separated by steppe and deserts from Khurasan and Transoxania, its closest sedentary neighbors, and thus retained its distinct identity. This identity was manifested in the use of the old Persian title of Khwarazm Shah, special dress, carts and patterns of rural settlement as well as a long tradition of de facto, if not always formalized, independence in both pre-Islamic and Islamic times. This tradition, together with the proximity of Khwarazm to the Qipchaq steppe (the region stretching between the Black Sea and the Caspian, also known as the Pontic steppe, after its main occupants from 1050, the Qipchaqs) with its ample nomadic population, made Khwarazm the most dangerous vassal of the Seljuqs. The region had been held since 1097 by a Turkish Mamluk of the Seljuqs, Anushtegin, whose sons eventually succeeded him. But it was only under his grandson Atsiz (1127–1156) that Khwarazm began to assert its independence. While nominally remaining loyal, Atsiz managed to enlarge considerably his territories in the Qipchaq steppe. He married the daughter of the Qipchaq Khan, added to his army many nomadic warriors of the Qipchaq and Qangli (the Qipchaqs' neighbors and relatives), and even tried to join forces with the Caliph against the Seljuqs. In 1141, after the Seljuq Sultan Sanjar was defeated by the Qara Khitai (whose attack was probably encouraged by Atsiz), the Khwarazm Shah chose to submit to the Qara Khitai. After that he skillfully used his alliance with the Qara Khitai to back his activity in the west, and took maximum advantage of Sanjar's difficulties with the Qarakhanids and the Oghuz tribesmen of Khurasan. After Sanjar's demise (1157) and the collapse of Seljuq power in the East, Atsiz's successors had even greater freedom of action. His grandson, Tekish Khwarazm Shah (1172–1200), who owed his crown to the Qara Khitai, directly challenged the Seljuqs, eliminating the last Seljuq Sultan in 1194, and adding Persia and 'Iraq al-'Ajam (western Iran) to his realm. After this victory, Tekesh expected the Abbasid Caliph to give him the same status the Seljuqs had enjoyed earlier. When the Caliph al-Nasir (1185–1225), who was striving to revive the authority of the Caliphate beyond Baghdad, refused, the Khwarazm Shah turned against him, a policy which was strengthened under Tekesh's son and successor, 'Ala' al-Din Muhammad (1200–1220), who had the unenviable task of facing Chinggis Khan.

The Mongols owed much to their immediate predecessors in the margins of the steppe, especially to their ability to combine nomad and sedentary territories and populations under effective rule. These states provided the Mongols with ready-made pools of officials, experienced in mediating foreign rule, officials who came either from among the indigenous bureaucrats and scribal classes of those states or, more commonly, from ex- (or post-) nomads who were already active (mainly as bureaucrats, governors or merchants) under the Mongols' predecessors. The important role of the ex-nomads, Uighurs, Khitans and, to a lesser extent, Khwarazmians and Khurasanians, in the ranks of the early Mongol empire certainly supports this notion.

Moreover, these nomadic or post-nomadic states still shared many features originating in nomadic political culture and social norms, which were quite close to those of the Mongols. They shared social values, such as the important role of warfare in everyday life, the high position of women and merchants, as well as elements of political culture, such as the importance of marriage alliances, the practice of hunting as a royal sport, the policy of holding hostages, and certain aspects of military organization. The position of women serves as a good example of this: in both Liao China and Seljuq and Khwarazm Central Asia we find noblewomen (mostly empresses and queens) involved in politics, taking part in military campaigns and sometimes leading their own considerable armies. This is in sharp contrast to the normative position of women in both China and the Muslim world, but it is very similar to the situation in Chinggis's Mongolia. Certainly the common nomadic culture facilitated Mongol rule over the steppe region and its sedentary margins.

Asia on the Eve of the Mongol Conquest

On the eve of Chinggis's rise, the political situation in Asia was rather complex. In the east, China was divided into three kingdoms: in the south was the ethnic-Chinese Song dynasty, by far the richest and technologically most advanced state of the time, but suffering from military weakness which obliged it to pay considerable tribute to its northern neighbor, the Jin dynasty. The Jurchen Jin dynasty ruled over Manchuria and most of northern China, relying on its huge military machine of both cavalry and infantry. By the late twelfth century the Jin were the superpower in the region of Mongolia, and their emperor, known in Mongolian as Altan Khan (the Golden Khan; *Jin* in Chinese means gold) was certainly the most prestigious ruler (see chapter two). Northwestern China, mainly the modern provinces of Gansu and Ninxia (and parts of Qinghai and Inner Mongolia), was ruled by the Xi Xia dynasty (1032–1227), of Tangut origin, a kingdom closer to Tibetan than to Chinese traditions, that left a rich Buddhist literature in its own

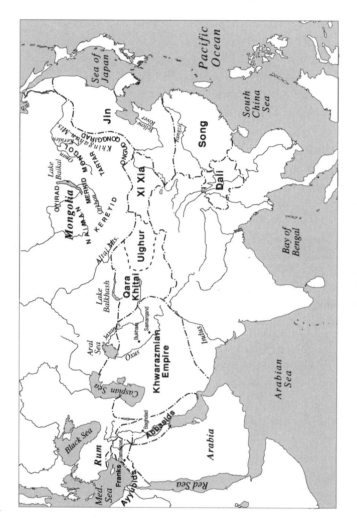

Map 2. Asia before Chinggis Khan

language and script. The semi-nomadic Tanguts ruled over a very hetero-geneous population, both ethnically and economically. One of the most important sources of income of their state was trade, as they were major mediators in the Silk Road trade between Central Asia and China, espe-cially after the dissolution of the Liao and the rise of the Jin. They were also one of the main sources of horses for the other China-based states.

West of the Tanguts lay the Qara Khitai empire described above. Once a flourishing and stable empire, by the early thirteenth century the Qara Khitai were plagued by problems of leadership and by power-seeking local governors and threatened as well by the ambitions of the Khwarazm Shah.

Behind the shrinking Qara Khitai empire was the newly established and quickly expanding Khwarizmian empire, by far the major Muslim power of the time, and yet troubled by weaknesses both personal and structural, as was soon exposed by the Mongol invasion. The reign of Muhammad Khwarazm Shah (1200–1220) saw both the height of Khwarazmian power and its rapid fall: Muhammad started his career by taking over the whole of Khurasan from the Ghurids (c. 1105–1215), a Persian dynasty centered in modern Afghanistan, which succeeded the Ghaznavids. With the help of the Qara Khitai in 1205 the Khwarazm Shah attacked the Ghurids, pushing them back into their Indian domains. Encouraged by this victory he turned against the Qara Khitai, taking over Transoxania in 1210 and eliminating the Qarakhanids and other local dynasties in 1212. In 1215 Muhammad eradicated the Ghurids, though some of their mamluks clung to power in India where they established the long-lasting Delhi sultanate (1210–1526). Intoxicated by his new power, and knowing that the Caliph had tried to incite both Ghurids and Qara Khitai against him, Muhammad then turned against the Abbasids. He took a most unusual step, denying Abbasid legitimacy and proclaiming an Alid as anti-Caliph, and then began a march on Baghdad. The snowstorms in the winter of 1217–18 halted his forces in Kurdistan and Luristan, and unrest among the Qipchaqs drove him back to Khwarazm where the Mongols soon demanded his full attention (see chapter three).

At the height of Khwarazm expansion, its territory reached to the frontier of the Caliph's lands. Despite the Khwarazmian attempts to dis-credit him, the Caliph was still a major symbol of legitimacy in the

Muslim world, but his actual rule did not go far beyond Iraq. Around him, several towns in al-Jazira (modern northern Iraq) and Iran were ruled by *atabeg* dynasties, remnants of the Seljuq period, and a Seljuq branch continued to rule in Anatolia (Rum) until 1307. Further westward, Egypt and Syria, parts of the Jazira and even eastern Anatolia were subject to the Ayyubids (1187–1250), heirs of Saladin, who never managed to restore the greatness of their founder. The Ayyubid princes fought among themselves and against the Franks, who maintained a foothold on the Syrian coast. The Caliph's reluctance to supply more than nominal support for the Muslim struggle against the infidel Crusaders was yet another source of tension in the already divided Muslim world of the early thirteenth century.

CONCLUSION

Two factors in late-twelfth- to early-thirteenth-century Asia favored the rise of Chinggis Khan. The first was the relative fragmentation of the political power in many parts of Eurasia: in the steppe, China and the Muslim world, there was no one central authority but rather multiple, competing dynasties, even though some, most notably the Jin and Song, were formidable military and economic powers.

The second factor was that most of these polities, especially those closest to the Mongols, were established by people of Inner Asian origin, mostly former nomads, who ruled over mostly sedentary but ethnically heterogeneous populations. These inter-regional states not only supplied precedents for nomadic conquest of sedentary realms but also provided models for a state in which a nomadic minority, backed by a strong nomadic army, ruled a heterogeneous, multi-ethnic and mixed nomadic-sedentary population. No doubt the nomadic social norms apparent in these states, rather similar to the Mongols' own, later contributed to the consolidation of Mongol rule.

These precedents notwithstanding, however, no one in the twelfth century could have predicted the rise of the Mongols from an obscure tribe to world conquerors. Nor would this have been possible without the leadership of Chinggis Khan.

2

TEMÜJIN'S MONGOLIA

Before the appearance of Chingiz Khan they had no chief or ruler. Each tribe or two tribes lived separately; they were not united with one another and there was constant fighting and hostility between them. Some of them regarded robbery and violence, immorality and debauchery as deeds of manliness and excellence. ... Their clothing was of skins of dogs and mice and their food was the flesh of those animals and other dead things; the sign of great emir amongst them was that his stirrups were of iron, from which one can form a picture of their other luxuries. And they continued in this indigence, privation and misfortune until the banner of Chingiz Khan's fortune was raised and they issued forth from the straits of hardship into the amplitude of well being.

Juwayni 1997, 21–22

A man is worthy of leadership who knows what hunger and thirst are and who can judge the condition of others thereby, who can go at a measured pace and not allow the soldiers to get hungry or thirsty or the horses to get worn out.

(words of wisdom of Chinggis Khan) Rashid/
Thackston 1999, 2: 296

God has spoken to me, saying: "I have given all the face of the earth to Temüjin and his children and I have named him Chingiz Khan"

Juwayni 1997, 39

The political fragmentation characteristic of much of Eurasia on the eve of Chinggis Khan's accession was found in twelfth-century Mongolia too. In fact, it took Chinggis more time and effort to unite the tribes of the eastern steppe than it took him to conquer half of the world. This chapter focuses on Temüjin's Mongolia and its tribal composition, and on his own tribe, the Mongols, their origin and early history. It then turns to the life of the young Chinggis himself, analyzing his spectacular rise to power, his enthronement in 1206 and the measures he took to reorganize Mongolian society, thereby laying the foundations for the future empire and for his great conquests.

THE TRIBAL COMPOSITION OF MONGOLIA

The Mongolia into which Temüjin, the future Chinggis Khan, was born was divided into several nomadic tribes, among whom Temüjin's ancestors held a rather marginal position. At the time of his birth, the three major tribes were the Tatar in eastern Mongolia, the Kereyid in the center, and the Naiman in the west.

The Tatars, old and bloody rivals of the Mongols, inhabited the steppe south of the Kerülen river, next to the Jin's northern frontiers. At the instigation of the Jin the Tatars often played an aggressive and active role in steppe politics, and had far more resources than neighboring tribes. Their name therefore become a generic appellation for the nomads of Mongolia and was later used as a synonym for Chinggis Khan's troops both in the Muslim world and in Europe. In Europe, the identification of the Mongols with the "Tartars" became widespread due to the similarity between the name Tatar and the word *tartarus*, a Latin word for hell.

West of the Tatars lived the Kereyids, a tribe of Turkic origin, whose core territory lay in the sacred realm of the Orkhon valley, a region which apart from its legitimating role also had strategic and economic importance, dominating the trade routes connecting Mongolia to China and western Asia. In the twelfth century the Kereyids professed Nestorian Christianity. They maintained close contacts with the Qara Khitai kingdom to their west and enjoyed a relatively stable leadership. As rivals of both Tatars and Naimans, they played a major role in Temüjin's rise to power.

West of the Kereyids, in the southern slopes of the Altai range and the upper course of the Irtish river, lived the Naiman, literally "The Eight," the last tribe to submit to Chinggis. The Naiman ruling family and nobility were of Turkic origin. They maintained close connections with their western neighbors, the Qara Khitai and the Uighurs, and borrowed from them some rudiments of statecraft such as the use of seals and of the Uighur script. Among the Naiman there were Buddhists and Nestorian Christians, though their leader was famed as a powerful shaman, specializing in weather magic.

Apart from these three major tribes several others deserve to be mentioned: northeast of the Naimans, in the lower course of the Selenga river, lived their allies, the Merkids. They were forest people in part, divided into three main branches, and generally did not posses a high degree of internal cohesion. North of the Merkids lived the forest tribes, most notable among them the Oyirad, rather marginal at the time of Chinggis's rise but destined for a celebrated history in the post-Chinggisid world. The forest people pursued a nomadic (though not pastoral) lifestyle in which hunting played a leading economic role. Although they often chose to remain neutral in the inter-tribal warfare in Mongolia, they were considered part of the manpower pool on which expanding steppe-based empires could draw.

Southeast Mongolia, across the Gobi, was the home of two other tribes, the Onggüd and the Qonggirad (also known as the Onggirad). The Onggüds, a Nestorian and Turkic-speaking tribe, resided along the Jin border with the Xi Xia, and considered themselves Jin vassals. Northeast of the Onggüds, on the western slope of the Great Khingan range, just west of the Mongols, lived the Qonggirad. This was the tribe from which the Mongols traditionally took their brides, a custom that continued after the founding of the empire.

The Mongols themselves lived in eastern Mongolia, between the Kerülen and the Onan rivers, north of their main enemies, the Tatars. According to their own tradition the Mongols originated from the union of a blue-gray wolf and a fallow doe, which took place at Burqan Qaldun, a mountain identified as one in the Khingan range where Chinggis Khan was later born. Chinggis Khan, however, was not a direct descendent of these mythological progenitors. One of their human descendants in the eleventh generation, Dobun, was married to Alan Qo'a (Alan the Fair) of the Qorolas tribe. After Dobun's death she was impregnated by Tengri, who appeared as a resplendent yellow man,

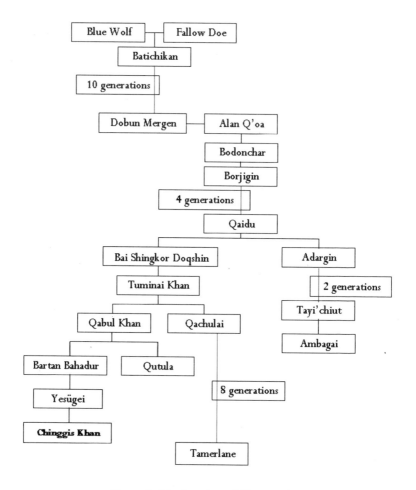

Figure 1. The Genealogy of Chinggis Khan

entering her tent through the smoke hole and departing on a moonbeam disguised as a yellow dog. Alan Qo'a then gave birth to three sons, the youngest of which, Bodonchar, founded the Borjigin clan, the senior Mongolian lineage into which Temüjin was born several generations later.

The name Mongol (Chinese: *Mengwu*) is first noted in the Chinese sources of the Tang dynasty (617–906) as a part of the Shiwei confederation. Subject first of the Turkic empire and later of the Khitan Liao, it was probably in the eleventh century that the Mongols migrated from northern Manchuria into eastern Mongolia. This migration was reflected in the Mongol epos as the one which brought the wolf and the doe to Burqan Khaldun, a tradition later retold in many Muslim sources. Qaidu, Alan Qo'a's great grandson and Chinggis's ancestor, was possibly active in late Liao times, but it is his great grandson and Chinggis's great grandfather, Qabul Khan, who is usually given credit for "ruling over all of the Mongols". Qabul's "state" is dated by Chinese sources to the mid twelfth century. Under his leadership the Mongols raided north China, and the Jin dynasty, acknowledging Qabul's authority over his followers, offered to grant him a tributary position if he stopped the raids. When invited to the court to conclude the details however, Qabul, drinking heavily, tweaked the Jin emperor's beard, an outrageous act which ended the negotiations, although Qabul managed to escape unharmed. The Jin were unable to avenge the insult, as Qabul died shortly after his return, but had their revenge in the reign of his heir, Ambaghai. A cousin of Qabul belonging to the Tayichi'ud clan, Ambaghai was chosen to replace Qabul and to lead the Mongols against their erstwhile rivals, the Tatars, who had then enjoyed Jin support. During the conflict the Tatars captured Ambaghai and dispatched him to the Jurchen court. There he was nailed to a wooden donkey and painfully bled to death. Ambaghai was succeeded by Qabul's third son, Qutula, thereby bringing Mongol leadership back to the Borjigin, Chinggis's clan. Qutula is described as a Mongol Hercules, but while he could break the back of a burly man as if he were an arrow shaft, he was less successful in the raids he mounted against the Tatars and the Jin, seeking revenge for Ambaghai. Nothing is known of his demise or the appointment of his successor: apparently with his death the Mongol polity fell apart. This disintegration can be dated to the early 1160s, namely around the time Chinggis Khan was born. The Mongols' early attempts at state formation did not leave a helpful legacy for Temüjin: Qabul, Ambaghai and Qutula were merely tribal war leaders who bequeathed no institutional foundations on which to build. Moreover, Chinggis's father, Yesügei, third son of Qabul's second son and a member of the newly-established Kiyad, a sub-clan of the Borjigin, did not have a prominent position among Mongol nobility. What Chinggis did inherit from this recent history was merely a double enmity, one towards the Jin, who had curtailed Mongol attempts at statehood, and another towards the Tatars, who were responsible for the death of Ambaghai. Later, they were to be responsible for the death of Chinggis's father too. Yet the lack of anything like a central government or even of a dominant tribe in Mongolia at this time, and the fluidity of the tribal structure deriving from this chronic political instability, created favorable circumstances for a talented young nomad to build up his own following.

TEMÜJIN'S YOUTH AND HIS RISE TO POWER

Contemporary Muslim and Chinese sources – with the notable exception of Rashid al-Din discussed below – are usually less informative about Chinggis Khan's early life than they are about his later conquests. Most of them mention the eastern origin of the Mongols, who resided on the fringes of North China; their submission to Altan Khan, the Jin emperor; the destitution and poverty prevailing among them before Chinggis's rise; as well as some general observations on the nomadic lifestyle of the Mongols, usually mentioning that "they had no religion," namely they did not adhere to any world religion. Chinggis Khan's youth and his rise to power are known mainly from the *Secret History of the Mongols*, the only surviving Mongol work of the thirteenth century, of which the chapters dealing with Chinggis are now usually dated to 1228. Another Mongol chronicle of the thirteenth century, the *Altan Debter* (Golden Book), did not survive, but we have both Chinese and Persian works based on it. The shorter, anonymous Chinese version is known as *Shengwu qinzheng lu* (Record of the Personal Campaigns of the Holy Warrior). It was written under Qubilai Khan (r. 1260–1294) and later served as a main source for the chapter on Chinggis Khan in the official history of the Mongol dynasty in China, the *Yuan shi*. The Persian version of the life and times of Chinggis Khan is narrated by Rashid al-Din (d. 1318), the greatest historian of the Mongols. Rashid al-Din, further discussed in chapters four and five, had access to the Mongol chronicle through oral transmission of Mongolian officials in Iran, where he served as one of the grand viziers of the Mongol rulers (ca. 1295–1318). To this he added information from earlier Muslim records, mainly the *History of the World Conqueror* by Juwayni, a Persian bureaucrat serving the Mongols (d. 1283) whose book is by far the most detailed report on Mongol conquests in the Muslim world and also a relatively elaborate record of Chinggis's early life. All three sources and especially the *Secret History* contain many legendary, mythical and folkloristic elements, yet they reflect the reality of nomadic life in thirteenth-century Mongolia. These three main sources, while sharing episodes, often contradict each other in terms of details and chronology, and only a very general outline of Temüjin's youth will be given below.[1]

Temüjin was probably born in 1162.[2] The eldest son of Yesügei and Hö'elun of the Qonggirad, he was called Temüjin (literally: blacksmith) after a Tatar chieftain killed by his father on the eve of his birth (calling newborns after recently vanquished enemies was a common nomadic custom). Temüjin was born holding a blood clot the size of a knuckle bone, a symbol of his future glory and of the bloodshed which accompanied it. He spent his early years near the Onan river, where he already found his first *anda*, Jamuqa, member of a different Mongol lineage, that of the Jadaran, who was due to become Temüjin's main rival for supremacy. When Temüjin was nine years old his father arranged his marriage to the daughter of the Qonggirad chief, the ten-year-old Börte, further cementing the ties between the two lineages. In accordance with Mongol custom, Temüjin remained with his in-laws, but not for long. His father, Yesügei, was poisoned by some Tatars during his return journey from the Qonggirat, and on his deathbed he summoned Temüjin back home. At the age of nine the orphaned Temüjin returned to his mother, only to find out that nobody wanted a nine-year-old chief.

---

[1] For a masterfully detailed (though not uncontested) reconstruction of Chinggis's life, see Ratchnevsky 1991; for a very compelling, albeit not always accurate, biography of Chinggis, see Weatherford 2004. I have drawn heavily on Allsen's chapter in Twitchett and Franke, 1994.

[2] The exact year is widely contested. I accept de Rachewiltz's chronology. A surprising source of support to this date (based on Chinese sources and accepted in Mongolia) is found in a seventeenth-century Muslim astronomical treatise from Quhistan. (See Kennedy 1991: 228). Other main alternatives are 1167 and 1155.

Most of Yesügei's followers went over to the rival clan, the Tayichi'ud, leaving Temüjin, his mother and brothers to their fate. This was the first but certainly not the last time Temüjin was betrayed by relatives, a fact that encouraged him to build his power base on non-kinsmen from an early age. At this stage, if we believe the *Secret History*, Temüjin and his family were on the verge of starvation, reduced to fishing and eating roots for sustenance. It was after a dispute over a fish that Temüjin and his brother, Jochi Qasar, killed their half-brother, Bekter, who had seized their catch. The issue at stake was more than a fish: Bekter was older than Temüjin, and though he was not a descendant of Yesügei's principal wife, he was a threat to Temüjin's primacy within the family. It is also possible that Temüjin killed Bekter to prevent him from marrying Temüjin's mother Hö'elun, for according to Mongol custom at the father's death his wives, except for the older son's mother, became the property of the eldest son. While fiercely rebuked by his mother for this act, Temüjin never expressed remorse. Here and afterwards, he was not to react lightly to affronts to his dignity. Soon thereafter, however, the rival Tayichi'ud, fearful of a possible threat from Yesügei's descendants, seized Temüjin. Had they killed him, world history would have looked different, but they merely enslaved him, fettering him in a wooden cangue and rotating him among their different families. After a while, with the help of a Tayichi'ud client, Temüjin managed to escape and reunite with his family. Yet life remained difficult and none too secure. The meager possessions of the family soon attracted bandits, who took the family's horses. Temüjin went out to retrieve them, returning in triumph and, at the same time, gaining his first *nöker*, Bo'orchu, who now joined him.

Encouraged by this first victory, Temüjin returned to the Qongirrad to ask for his bride. The Qonggirad remembered their alliance with Yesügei and thus were willing to end the isolation of Chinggis's family. They gave him Börte as well as a magnificent sable coat as her wedding present. With this coat Temüjin, again building on his father's legacy, tried to secure an alliance with one of the major tribes of Mongolia. Sometime in 1183/4, he approached Toghril, later known as Ong Khan, the leader of the Kereyids, and Yesügei's *anda*. Softened by the precious gift, and remembering Yesügei's help against his own family's attempts to dethrone him, Toghril accepted Temüjin as his adopted son and promised help. Indeed, Toghril's mere acknowledgment led to an increase in Temüjin's followers. Toghril, moreover, was soon asked to give aid when the Merkids attacked Temüjin's camp. Temüjin managed to escape, but the Merkids kidnapped his wife in retaliation for Yesügei's former abduction of Temüjin's mother from the Merkid chief. The kidnapping of women was rather common in Mongolia – especially among those who could not afford to pay the bride price – and did not necessarily require immediate retaliation. Temüjin, however, thought differently. He called on all his allies, including Toghril, who had his own score to settle with the Merkids, and Temüjin's own *anda*, Jamuqa, who was allied with the Kereyids at this stage. With their help, Temüjin moved against the Merkid. His reunion with Börte, who ran into his arms on recognizing his voice, is one of the most touching episodes in the *Secret History* (and one often retold in folktales, romances and, later, films). Börte, however, came back heavily pregnant. Although she had spent nearly nine months among the Merkids, Chinggis always regarded her first-born, Jochi (literally: guest, visitor) as his own son, but others had their doubts about Jochi's paternity, and these doubts played a role in depriving Jochi of a chance of succeeding his father. On a more practical level, the battle against the Merkids was Temüjin's first victory on the field, through which he began to make a name for himself as a war leader.

After this great victory Temüjin camped for a year and a half with Jamuqa. In this period he gained a sizable following, attracting more and more kinsmen and *nökers* to his side, and acquiring further military experience. His exceptional military talents and growing popularity, however, soon made him a competitor of Jamuqa. Following the advice of his wife, and after the hated Tayichi'ud chose to align with Jamuqa, Temüjin decided to separate from his *anda*. He moved into the upper Kerülen, where around 1186 his uncles, perhaps seeing him as less dangerous than Jamuqa, enthroned him as khan of the Mongol tribe. While Temüjin actually ruled mainly the Borjigin clan, since neither the Tayichiu'd nor the Jadaran were subject to his authority, the enthronement nonetheless greatly enhanced his authority and prestige. The new khan organized a household establishment, appointing his *nökers* as cooks, herders, quiver bearers, waggoneers and chamberlains, thereby creating the kernel of his future imperial guard. This rise in his position, while welcomed by Ong Khan, alienated Jamuqa, who attacked Temüjin in 1187, a clash which resulted in the one and only decisive defeat the future Chinggis Khan ever suffered in the field. Temüjin's political wisdom (and Jamuqa's lack of it) enabled him, however, to turn this defeat into victory. Making full use of the exceptional cruelty with which Jamuqa treated his opponents – he boiled seventy princes in large cauldrons – Temüjin managed to convince many of Jamuqa's supporters to desert their master and join his camp. However, it is possible that the battle had taken a heavy toll on Temüjin,[3] for we know nothing of his whereabouts until 1196, when we find him fighting against the Tatars. Perhaps, as Ratchnevsky has suggested, Temüjin spent some of this time in Jin captivity. This period seemed to have been a trial also for Temüjin's main ally, Toghril. Being threatened by his brothers, Toghril had to find refuge in the Qara Khitai realm, and Temüjin was instrumental in restoring him to power when he had returned from his exile, probably around 1195 to 1196.[4] In 1196, however, both Temüjin and Toghril fought against the Tatars with the Jin's encouragement. Apparently, the Jin wanted to build up Kereyid authority as a counterweight to the Tatars, thereby giving Temüjin and Toghril an opportunity to avenge themselves on their long-time enemies. Following their victory, the Jin gave Toghril the title of Ong Khan (Chinese *wang*, prince), while Temüjin received the lesser title of *j'aut- quri* (Khitan: commander of hundreds). This battle marked the beginning of a series of feuds among the tribes of Mongolia in which Temüjin and Ong Khan most often stood together, raiding groups of Naiman and Merkid, while Temüjin also brought into line Mongol lineages such as the Jürkin, who defied his leadership.

The ongoing success of Temüjin and Ong Khan prompted Jamuqa, now an open enemy, to forge his own coalition. In 1201 an alliance of lesser tribes enthroned Jamuqa as Gürkhan (universal khan). Choosing the title so far used in Mongolia only by the Kereyid (and originating in

[3] Rashid al-Din ascribed the cauldrons' episode to Chinggis himself.

[4] The dating of Ong Khan's escape to the Qara Khitai and his restoration are still in dispute. Cf. Togan 1998; Ratchnevsky 1991 and de Rachewiltz 2004, who dated it to between 1198–1201.

the Qara Khitai realm) was a direct challenge to Ong Khan's leadership. Both Toghril and Temüjin moved against Jamuqa. Ong Khan inflicted a heavy defeat on him which led Jamuqa to plunder the camps of his own followers, further fracturing his coalition. Temüjin's main aim in this campaign was the Tayichiu'd, Jamuqa's supporters and his former tormentors. Subduing them on the Tula river, despite being seriously wounded in action, he systematically executed their leaders and incorporated the people into his own following. The Tayichi'ud were broken once and for all, and as a bonus Temüjin received the allegiance of one of their clients, Jebe, who turned out to be one of his most brilliant generals. In addition the Qnggirad, his wife's tribe and a former ally of Jamuqa, also chose to submit. Although Jamuqa's power was not yet completely broken, the victory greatly increased the prestige and authority of both Ong Khan and Temüjin.

Temüjin used his growing power to settle scores with the Tatars. After resting his troops, the Mongols, without the Kereyids, attacked the Tatars in the autumn of 1202 at their pastures near the Khalkha river. Before the battle Temüjin had ordered his troops to refrain from plunder until victory was assured, a rule strictly enforced from that day onward. The battle resulted in a crushing defeat for the Tatars, and Temüjin ordered that all the male Tatars taller than the linchpin of a cart (i.e. above two feet) should be executed, and that the rest should be divided amongst his troops. Only women and children now survived from the Mongols' major enemy, once the dominant tribe in Mongolia; Yesügei's death was avenged.

After this great victory, Temüjin controlled all of eastern Mongolia, his power nearly equaling that of Ong Khan. This required an adjustment in their relationship. Ong Khan suggested appointing his promising adopted son as his legitimate heir. Temüjin accepted and as a means of further cementing the alliance asked for the latter's granddaughter as a wife for his eldest son. The father of the bride-to-be, Ong Khan's son Senggüm, refused. Envious of Temüjin's success, and coveting his father's throne for himself, he convinced the aging Kereyid leader that Temüjin was undermining his authority and had to be killed. Jamuqa, who had apparently improved his relations with the Kereyids since 1201, also played a part in persuading Ong Khan to betray his adopted son. Planning to lure Temüjin to a feast where he could assassinate him,

Senggüm informed him that he agreed to the wedding. Temüjin went out toward the Kereyid camp unsuspecting, but was warned in the last moment by two loyal shepherds. He managed to escape, but was forced to run away with only a few followers. Taking refuge near the river or lake of Baljuna, probably south of the Khalkha in southeast Mongolia, Temüjin saw his life-long enterprise on the verge of collapse. Yet he was moved by the fidelity of those who stayed with him during this period of trial. Together they drank from the bitter water of Baljuna and swore to share both the bitter and the sweet consequences of the task ahead. Having been present at Baljuna later conferred high honor on the participants. Those who remained with Temüjin at this time were an extremely heterogeneous group: Khitans from northern China, Tanguts, Muslim traders from Central Asia, and perhaps also Indians. It also included Kereyid and Naiman, but not one Mongol apart from Temüjin and his brother Jochi Qasar, again proving the supremacy of personal loyalty over kinship. For our purposes, the important thing is that it was in Baljuna that for the first time Muslims began to play a role in the life of Chinggis Khan.

Gradually, however, more Mongol contingents rejoined Temüjin. Still outnumbered, he went against the Kereyids, the battle causing heavy casualties on both sides. Temüjin let his troops rest for the summer, trying to enlist as many allies as possible, including many Kereyid defectors, for the decisive showdown with Ong Khan. In the autumn of 1203 the Mongols launched a counter attack, overwhelming their rivals after a bitter three-day battle. Ong Khan, who had escaped into Naiman territory, was killed by their guard who refused to believe that the pitiable old man before them was the famous Kereyid leader, while Senggüm (son of Ong Khan) fled southward into the Xi Xia realm. Temüjin was relatively generous to his defeated enemies, forgiving their commanders, marrying Kereyid princesses to his sons and dividing their troops amongst his army. Eastern and central Mongolia was now under his control, including the strategic and sacred realm of the Orkhon valley. Many Muslim sources suggest that his supremacy in Mongolia began at this stage.

The new situation also meant that Temüjin's domains now bordered on the territory of the Naiman, the major tribe in western Mongolia. In

1204 Chinggis Khan moved against them in what was to be his last decisive battle before the unification of Mongolia. The threatened Naiman Khan proposed an alliance to the Onggüds in order to attack the Mongols simultaneously from two fronts, but the Onggüds preferred to submit to Temüjin. The Naimans still had an alliance with the Merkids and with Jamuqa's clan, the Jadaran. Temüjin took great care in planning this battle, appointing his first bodyguard (*kesig*) before launching the attack. Aware of his numerical inferiority, he also ordered his vanguard to light fires at night, thereby creating the impression they had a much bigger force than they actually had, a trick often used in later Mongol campaigns. The two armies met near the Altai mountains, where the Naiman coalition suffered a major defeat. All the Naimans who survived the onslaught were incorporated into the Mongol army. In addition, a number of tribes that accompanied the Naimans also chose to submit.

With the demise of Tayang Khan of the Naiman, Temüjin's only serious rival in Mongolia remained Jamuqa. The latter fled from the battlefield but was soon captured by his own people, who handed him to Temüjin. Temüjin executed them for betraying their master, but subsequently, in 1205, also put to death his former *anda*. Although Merkid and Naiman elements continued to resist and the forest tribes were still to be subjugated, Temüjin was now the uncontested lord of Mongolia. To formalize his status, a Grand Assembly (Mongolian: *quriltai*) was summoned in the spring of 1206 to the source of the Onan river, where the tribes of Mongolia invited Temüjin to be their leader. His white battle standard with the nine flying yak tails was raised, and the shaman Teb Tengri installed him as Chinggis Khan.

The etymology and meaning of the title Chinggis Khan have been long and fiercely debated. The two leading opinions are those of Pelliot, who argues for the meaning of Oceanic, hence universal, Khan (from *Tenkiz*, Turkic: Ocean), and de Rachewiltz, who supports the meaning of mighty, strong, or firm Khan (from *ching*, Mongolian: hard, strong). But whatever its literal meaning, the title obviously implied superiority over other rulers. Moreover, unlike Gürkhan, the similar-meaning title chosen by Jamuqa or Ong Khan, Chinggiz Khan was a completely new title, so that its adoption signaled the beginning of a new era.

Several factors, apart from his well-attested military talent, contributed to Chinggis's rise to prominence in Mongolia. First was his political skill, making the best out of any alliance available to him – whether by marriage or *anda* – and not hesitating to turn against former allies when the need arose, usually after blaming them for betraying him.

A second factor was Temüjin's "egalitarian" policy: he treated his rank and file well, dressed his people in his own clothes, allowed them to ride his own horses, and let them eat the same food as he ate himself. Treating his soldiers "as if they are my brothers," Chinggis never required them to undertake tasks beyond their physical abilities and never allowed their commanders to beat them. Furthermore, he distributed the booty equally among all the participants in the raid, securing shares even for the widows and orphans of those who perished in the battle. Chinggis thereby acquired a reputation for generosity, a highly regarded trait in nomadic societies. In return for fair treatment he demanded full devotion and obedience, and whoever failed in this was harshly punished. Still, the rules were clear and the rewards for loyalty were equal to the punishments for disobedience. Moreover, given his frequent disappointment in his kinsmen and the fact that he came from a relatively minor lineage in his tribe, Chinggis did not ascribe much importance to people's descent or to their position in the tribal hierarchy but rather to their individual talents and loyalty. This policy presented people of humble origin a unique opportunity to rise to prominence in his newly assembled troops, and they flocked to his side.

Another factor contributing to Temüjin's success was his widely attested personal appeal. Even as a child Chinggis had an imposing appearance, his future father-in-law being impressed by the "flashing eyes and lively face" of the nine-year-old Temüjin. As a man Chinggis was distinguished by his height: he was powerfully built and had "cat-like" eyes. His appearance and qualities attracted many to his side, and not a few of his first adherents were envoys or merchants employed by others who chose to stay in his service.

Chinggis Khan's unique qualifications as administrator and organizer, another major reason for his success, were clearly manifest after he had united the Mongol tribes in the *quriltai* of 1206.

INSTITUTIONAL CHANGES: MONGOLIA IN TRANSITION

Several Muslim sources, perhaps anachronistically but in accord with modern anthropological theories, relate that the Mongols enthroned Chinggis Khan under pressure from an external threat, either the Jin or (much less plausibly) the Khwarazm Shah. Turning outside against enemies could have also supplied additional sources of wealth for Chinggis's supporters. Yet despite these economic and political conditions, the first task Chinggis Khan turned to during the 1206 *quriltai* and in the whole incubation period of 1204–9 was the reorganization of Mongolia's nomadic society. Well aware of the fluidity of alliances which played such a pivotal role in his rise to power, Chinggis took measures to ensure a much more centralized, political-military system before launching major raids, carefully laying the foundations for the nascent Mongol empire. The *Secret History* devotes much space to the administrative arrangements and the lists of nominations, thereby attesting to their importance. The focus of this reorganization was the army, the judicial system and the religiously inspired ideology.

The reorganization of the army was one of the most revolutionary acts of Chinggis Khan and a major reason for his future success. Moreover, since every Mongol was a soldier, the military reorganization meant also a dramatic social change, breaking up the traditional tribal configuration. Under Chinggis Khan, the whole manpower of Mongolia was reorganized into decimal-based military units of 10, 100, 1000 and 10,000. The unit of one thousand (Mongolian: *mingghan*) was the basic structural element of the army. Ten *mingghan* were grouped to form a *tümen*, unit of 10,000, only when the need arose, and a commander of one of the *mingghan* was entrusted with the leadership of the larger formation, although he also continued to lead his own thousand. The decimal organization was a traditional Inner-Asian institution, but while the pre-Chinggisid decimal units were organized along tribal lines and led by the tribal chief, Chinggis's units were composed of many tribes, and at their head stood his loyal followers, the *nökers*. Tribes which had peacefully submitted to the rising Chinggis, such as the Onggüd, the Qonggirad, the Oyirad, or the Jalayir, retained some of their integrity, providing whole units of a thousand, but opposition tribes such as the Kereyid, Tatar, Merkid, and Naiman – or what was left of them – were broken up and distributed among the different units. The soldier's unit became his new focus of identity, and the commanders replaced the tribal chief as the new nobility of the Mongols. The soldier's loyalty was now to his unit commander and to the latter's commander, Chinggis Khan. Chinggis used this opportunity to reward his loyal followers, personally nominating each of the 95 commanders of a thousand. Many *nökers* rose to power in 1206 from the lowest ranks of shepherds, stewards, or even carpenters. The physical extermination of most of Mongolian tribal nobility during Chinggis's rise to power facilitated the completion of this revolution.

Over and above the ordinary military formations, Chinggis created his imperial guard (*kesig*). At 10,000 men strong in 1206, the guard became a fundamental institution of the Mongolian state, fulfilling several key functions. The guard was responsible for the Khan's personal security, guarding his tent in shifts day and night. It also took care of the Khan's well-being, comprising officers responsible for his food and drink, garments, weapons, and herds as well as for writing his decrees and recording his deeds. In addition, the guard had police functions, apprehending thieves and enforcing order, and served also as the elite troops of the Mongols. The *kesig* was recruited from the decimal units, whose commanders were asked to assign both their sons and their best warriors to it, regardless of their genealogy. The *kesig* therefore served as both a reservoir of hostages, an additional insurance for the commanders' loyalty (sons of subject rulers were later added to this reservoir), and as a training center for future Mongol commanders endowed with good genes or proven quality, and often both. Most of Chinggis's leading generals, including Jebe, Sübedei and Muqali (mentioned in the next chapter), soon to be sent across Asia, grew up in the ranks of the *kesig*. Being a member of the *kesig* was highly prestigious, and indeed it was the nursery of the new ruling class of the Mongol empire, both on the field and outside it, and the nucleus of much of its future central administration.

Chinggis Khan also fixed specific regulations for ensuring the smooth management of his new state. These included the duties and rights of commanders and soldiers, notably forbidding transfers among units and imposing strict discipline; rules regarding military training through hunting; and the basics of penal law. These regulations, which continued to evolve throughout Chinggis's life and afterwards, and were allegedly recorded by the guardsmen, probably served as the basis for the famous Grand *Jasaq* (usually known in its Turkish form, *Yasa*), the legal code ascribed to Chinggis Khan, which is one of the most disputed subjects in the study of Mongol history.[5] The *Jasaq* is considered to be one of Chinggis's greatest achievements, because, albeit probably encompassing much of the former Mongol customary law, it was at least partly invented by Chinggis "from the page of his own mind without the toil of pursuing records or the trouble of confirming with tradition" (Juwaynī 1997: 23–4). Chinggis therefore was not only the enforcer, but also the giver of law.

The common wisdom in the research literature till the 1980s was that at the 1206 *quriltai* Chinggis gave his followers a coherent legal code, the *Jasaq*, to mark the foundation of his new polity. As David Ayalon and David Morgan have shown, however, this is not supported by the sources. Part of the problem derives from the fact that *jasaq* in Mongolian means both law or legal code and an individual order or act of law, and the scattered references in the *Secret History* (none of them related to the 1206 *quriltai*) seem to refer to specific orders, not to a comprehensive legal code. Moreover, no copy of the *Jasaq* survived, and no historian ever claimed to have read it. It would seem that the *Jasaq* in a coherent form was put into writing only in the reign of Chinggis's heir, Ögödei, who is described in Chinese sources as promulgating it during his accession ceremony. Even though it is impossible to restore the full content of the *Jasaq*, obviously the Mongols of the thirteenth century and afterwards (and many of their subjects and neighbors) believed that it existed and knew what it intended. The *Jasaq* seemed to have been an adaptable and dynamic code, which continued to evolve after Chinggis's time and into which his various successors added their own regulations (for the *Jasaq*'s later relationship with the Muslim law, the *shari'a*, see

[5] For the *Jasaq* see Morgan 2005; deRachewiltz 1993; Aigle 2004. I basically follow Morgan.

chapter four). Yet Chinggis Khan was always considered the source of the *Jasaq* and the origin of its sanctions.

But while Chinggis did not create a comprehensive legal code in the 1206 *quriltai*, he did establish a juridical authority meant to enforce the new order and supervise its administration. He appointed his adopted brother or son, the Tatar Shigi Qutuqu, to be the chief judge (*yeke yarghuchi*) of the Mongols. Shigi Qutuqu, helped by several of the night guards, was to arbitrate in disputes, try evildoers, and divide and apportion subject people and later also appanages. He was also asked to register his decisions – and Chinggis's legal decrees – in a blue register, thereby creating a body of precedents for future use, perhaps another foundation for the *Jasaq*. The mere idea of record keeping was another of Chinggis's innovations: in 1204, following the battle with the Naiman, and under their influence, Chinggis adopted the Uighur script for writing Mongolian. Literacy, certainly, was an asset in administrating a state and, later, empire and soon became an important criterion for promotion and advancement. And it was used for other purposes as well: the first surviving specimen of Mongolian writing records the winner in an archery match from 1225.

Apart from reorganizing the army and the juridical system, Chinggis also took measures to strengthen his political-religious ideology, which became a major source of his legitimacy. The heavenly mandate which the shaman Teb Tengri conferred upon Chinggis during the 1206 *quriltai* had deep roots in the steppe (as discussed in chapter one). Just as in the case of the Turkic empire, however, the world over which Teb Tengri enthroned Chinggis was the world of the dwellers of the felt tents, namely the world of Mongolia and of the steppe. Chinggis, however, made two important changes in this concept. First, after the series of successful conquests discussed in chapter three, he broadened the mandate realm from the world of the steppe to the entire world. Second, already during the incubation period following his coronation, he diminished the shaman's role as the link between the ruler and heaven, replacing it with his own direct and personal connection to Tengri.

The replacing of Teb Tengri arose not for reasons of doctrine but of politics. Teb Tengri, aware of his power as the voice of Heaven, first tried to sow dissention within Chinggis's family, noting that Heaven considered transferring the mandate to Chinggis's brother, Jochi Qasar. Only the intervention of their mother saved Jochi Qasar from Chinggis's wrath. Teb Tengri, however, continued to gather around him those dissatisfied with Chinggis's reforms, breaching his newly instituted regulations by encouraging people assigned to Chinggis's younger brother, Temüge, to desert their units and join him. Chinggis decided that the feud between the shaman and his brother would be settled in a traditional wrestling match. According to his orders, however, his brother stationed three strong men outside the Khan's tent, and before the match started they seized Teb Tengri and broke his spine. Chinggis declared that the shaman's fate was the will of heaven. While he had appointed another shaman (of a smaller tribe) and continued to use the services of astrologers and diviners throughout his rule, by eliminating the noted shaman Chinggis Khan asserted not only the primacy of imperial power over that of the priests – as accepted in East Asian traditions – but also his close and personal relation to Heaven.

Chinggis's intimate connection with the supernatural is stressed in both Mongolian and Muslim sources. Major manifestations of this connection are the Khan's super-human origin; his skill in magic, deception and scapulimancy (divination by interpreting cracks in the burned shoulder bones of sheep); and also his consultations with Tengri before taking important decisions. These were highly personal consultations, made sometimes on a high mountain or after several days of prayers; the victories that followed were accordingly ascribed to Tengri's support. By placing himself in a shaman's position, Chinggis Khan enhanced the sacral component of his leadership, bolstering his prestige among the Mongols.

While simultaneously organizing his realm and consolidating his legitimacy, Chinggis continued to work toward securing his hold in Mongolia. The main opposition came from the remnants of the Naiman-Merkid coalition, and campaigns against them had already begun on a small scale in 1206. In 1208, a year after subjugating the forest tribes, Chinggis moved against the Naiman-Merkid coalition with full force, crushing them near the Irtish river. The Merkid leader was slain, though some princes fled westwards to the Uighur realm, while the Naiman prince Güchülüg took refuge in the Qara Khitai domains. This victory not only gave Chinggis fame outside Mongolia, but also demonstrated the superiority of his newly centralized army over the rival tribal levies. However, even when most of his energy was turned toward the outside world (as will be discussed in the next chapter), Chinggis still took precautions to defend his rear. Only the series of victorious conquests outside Mongolia convinced even its most stubborn tribesmen that they would be better off by remaining under Chinggis Khan's standard.

Unifying Mongolia was a long and tortuous process, but Chinggis learnt its lessons. Determined to avoid the fluidity of the tribal alliances, he chose to devote a few years to creating a new, more centralized, structure for his state. This consolidation period established a firm infrastructure for his future conquests and rule.

3

WORLD CONQUEST: HOW DID HE DO IT?

Never had anything like it been heard of. Even Alexander [The Great] who all sources agree in saying was the ruler of the world did not come to dominate it so rapidly, but needed ten years to do so; he did not kill anyone but was content with the submission of the people. But in just one year [the Mongols] seized the most populous, the most beautiful and the best cultivated parts of earth whose inhabitants excelled in character and urbanity. In the countries that have not yet been overrun by them, everyone spends the night afraid that they may appear there too.

Ibn al-Athir 1966: 12:235, cited in Spuler 1972: 31

There is nothing surprising in the fact that after 1206 Chinggis Khan commenced preparations for attacks on his sedentary neighbors: the natural course of action for a newly established nomadic empire was to turn outward. This supplemented the nomadic economy by acquiring riches from its sedentary neighbors, allowed the leader to reward his followers and therefore consolidate his position, and focused the energies of his followers on external objectives, thereby deflecting attention from internal differences. What is surprising is that Chinggis Khan was far more successful than any nomadic chief before or after: he died ruling over the largest territory a single man had ever conquered – from northern China to the Caspian sea, from Afghanistan to the fringes of Siberia. This chapter reviews Chinggis Khan's campaigns, stressing the gradual transition from raiding to conquest, and consider the internal consolidation of the empire, trying to explain the unusual success of Chinggis Khan (and his descendants), with special reference to the role of the Muslim world in his rise to unprecedented power. Four issues are crucial in this regard: the organization and strategies of the army, including the calculated use of devastation; the willingness to learn from foreigners; Chinggis' political skills; and success itself, an important element in nomadic political ideology.

THE CONQUESTS

If the natural course for Chinggis Khan was external expansion, the natural direction was China, the time-honored objective of the nomads from the Mongolian steppes. Among the three contemporary Sinitic states, Chinggis decided to start with the smallest – and weakest – the Tangut Xi Xia empire, a good but not-too-dangerous test for his newly-assembled troops. Attacking the Xi Xia had other advantages: first, the Tanguts were allies of the Jin; subduing them would therefore deprive the Jin of an important ally in later confrontations with the Mongols and enable Chinggis Khan to secure his western flank. Second, the Tanguts controlled a significant part of the Silk Road trade and were therefore important for securing Mongol participation in this ongoing commerce. On a more personal level, the Xi Xia had given refuge to many Kereyid

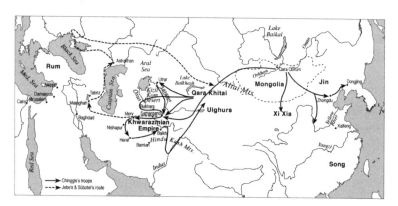

Map 3. Chinggis Khan's Campaigns of Conquest

leaders, most recently Ong Khan's son, Senggüm, a rival of Chinggis Khan. Although Senggüm soon fled the Xi Xia domain southward (only to be killed a few years later by Turks from India), the Tanguts were still guilty of sheltering Mongol refugees. Indeed, revenge and the elimination of potential rivals are the apparent motivations for Chinggis Khan's first campaigns, much more so than any grand design for world conquest.

The attacks on the Tanguts began by raids on their territories in 1205, 1207 and, on a more massive scale, from 1209 onward. In 1211 these raids resulted in Xi Xia's submission. The Tanguts agreed to give the Mongols a significant tribute of camels, brocade and gyrfalcons, to end their alliance with the Jin, and to provide, when required, auxiliary troops for the Mongol army. To cement the deal Chinggis Khan obtained a Tangut princess to marry. Conquest was not the goal at this stage, and the Mongols, satisfied for the moment, returned home. Mongol success against the Tanguts was not overlooked by the Central Asian powers to the West: in 1209 the Uighur ruler, well aware of the growing Mongol power from their vigorous pursuit of the Merkid who had fled into his territories in 1208, and until then a vassal of the Qara Khitai, transferred his allegiance to Chinggis Khan. This was the first submission of a sedentary polity to the Mongols and the Uighur ruler, receiving a Chinggisid princess in marriage, was declared Chinggis's fifth son. Thus begun a fruitful relationship between the two peoples as the Uighurs remained important cultural brokers for the Mongols throughout the period of the united empire (1206–1260) and beyond.

Following the Uighurs, another Qara Khitai vassal submitted to Chinggis Khan in 1211. This was Arslan Khan, leader of the Qarluqs of Qayaliq (in modern south-eastern Kazakhstan), who became the first Muslim ruler to join the Mongols. The ruler of Almaliq, a neighboring Muslim city also previously under Qara Khitai rule, soon followed. For Chinggis Khan, however, the main implication of the Tangut submission and that of their western neighbors was that it enabled him to attack the Jurchen Jin dynasty in northern China.

Chinggis had many reasons to challenge the Jin. First, as the neighboring superpower, it was only to be expected that Jin would continue its traditional policy of inciting one steppe tribe against another, in order to undermine the newly-achieved unity in Mongolia. Jin's war with the

Song in 1206–8 and the subsequent succession struggle and internal unrest delayed the Jurchen reaction to the rise of Chinggis Khan, but in 1210 the Jurchen emissaries returned to Mongolia, demanding that Chinggis pay tribute to Altan Khan. This was of course another bone of contention: theoretically Chinggis was still a vassal of Jin, an intolerable position for someone with his ambitions. In addition, Chinggis had several old grudges against the Jin: a historical one, relating to the Jurchen execution of his ancestor Ambaghai, and a more recent one, because the newly enthroned Jurchen emperor (Weishao Wang 1209–1213) had insulted him while he was bringing tribute to the Jin. Beyond this, the riches of the Jin were a perfect source of booty for rewarding his troops. No wonder then that when Jin envoys came in 1210 to inform him of Weishao Wang's enthronement and to ask for tribute, Chinggis spat in their face and prepared for war.

In 1211, after leaving a considerable force to secure his rear in Mongolia, Chinggis Khan advanced southwards toward Jin territory. He had already gathered much information about the Jin situation, both from allied merchants and from Chinese, Jurchen and especially Khitan turncoats who chose to join him before or during the campaign. The Mongols advanced in two columns, the eastern one led by Chinggis and the western by his trusted general Jebe. Jin border fortifications (not to be confused with the Great Wall of China, which did not exist at the time) were crossed without problem since their defenders, the Onggüds, had already submitted to Chinggis Khan. The troops under Chinggis's command defeated the elite troops of the Jin, while Jebe's forces took the strategic Juyong mountain pass guarding the Jin central capital, Zhongdu (modern Beijing), his troops preventing Jin garrisons stationed on the Xi Xia border from coming to the aid of their capital. The Mongols ravaged and plundered the countryside around the city, without, however, attacking the city itself. In the winter of early 1212 the Mongols withdrew northward, either because Chinggis Khan suffered an injury, or simply because they had all the booty they could carry off.

The Jin regained the pass and much of their lost territories, but in the fall of 1212 the Mongols returned. They took the Juyong pass, this time with the help of Ja'far Khwaja, a Muslim merchant and a veteran of Baljuna. Familiar with the region from his commercial travels, Ja'far guided the Mongol troops at night through a narrow mountainous path and, when Jin soldiers woke up the next morning, they were taken completely by surprise. This time the Mongols penetrated much deeper into Jin territory. Divided into three columns, they wrought havoc in the agricultural lands north of the Yellow River, and blockaded Zhongdu. Despite the desire of his generals to annihilate the Jin, Chinggis preferred to conclude with peace. This was because the main goal of this campaign was still booty and because the siege was taking a heavy toll on his troops. In addition, while he was already building up a force of siege engineers, Chinggis was not yet confident in his troops' ability to assault a heavily fortified city such as Zhongdu. The peace agreement, negotiated by Ja'far and rather similar to the one concluded with the Tanguts, secured the Mongols plenty of gold, silk and horses, accompanied by a Jurchen princess. The Mongols lifted the siege and rode northward.

Immediately after signing the peace agreement, in summer 1214, the panic-stricken Jin court chose to take a traditional Chinese step and transferred its capital further to the interior, in this case to Kaifeng on the Yellow river, where they thought they would be well beyond the reach of the Mongol army. Chinggis saw this move as a deliberate violation of the agreement, and he ordered his troops to renew the siege. Zhongdu held for eight months, after Mongol attempts to take it by storm failed. In May 1215, after the city's population, reduced to cannibalism, had lost all hope, the Mongols entered Zhongdu. The end of the siege was followed by a week of carnage and pillage, which allegedly left the streets of the Jin capital greasy from human fat.

Simultaneously, another Mongol force advanced to the northeast, along the Manchurian coast. The Jurchen homeland was already in turmoil, as many Jin generals, sensing the dynasty's weakness, had tried to carve out their own ephemeral kingdoms. Some of the Jin generals were not ethnically Jurchen and the Mongols, at this stage enthusiastically incorporating the petty kings, fully exploited their grudges against the Jin. By far the most important allies the Mongols gained in Manchuria at that point were the Khitans, remnants of the Liao dynasty destroyed earlier by the Jin. Submitting *en masse* in 1215, the Khitans played a pivotal role in the subsequent subjugation of northern China and in the early Mongol administration. By 1216 a large part of the Jurchen homeland was already in Mongol hands, and the Jin dynasty, deprived of its central capital, was on the verge of collapse. At this stage, however, Chinggis Khan left Muqali, a trusted general, in charge of the ongoing small-scale operation against the Jin (which Muqali continued till his death in 1223), while the Great Khan and his army turned back to face the new challenges from the west. This time, however, Chinggis Khan left governors and garrisons behind. The conquest had begun.

The change from raiding to conquest at this stage was tactical, not strategic, dictated by battlefield conditions and by Jin behavior. The Jurchens proved they were unreliable in keeping peace agreements, and therefore Chinggis Khan sought their complete destruction, a goal that could best be achieved by leaving governors and garrisons in Zhongdu as a base for further operations. It was also at this stage that the Mongols, under Muqali's direction, systematically begun to collect and allocate "useful people," e.g. artisans and military technologists from northern China, in addition to using conquered peoples in their army. Yet by conquering northern China, although deviating from the custom of former steppe empires in Mongolia, Chinggis Khan can be seen as following the Liao and Jin pattern, namely aiming to create another East Asian state of nomadic origin. The change into a real world empire began only after Mongol involvement in the Muslim world.

What made Chinggis turn westward was a challenge to his leadership of the Mongol world. First, the forest tribes of north-western Mongolia rebelled again, and in 1216 Chinggis Khan sent his generals to subdue them completely. In the same year he also dispatched his loyal general, Jebe, to cope with a more serious challenge which arose further westward, in the lands of the Qara Khitai. In 1208, when Chinggis had fought the Merkid and Naiman tribes, one Naiman prince, Güchülüg, escaped into the Qara Khitai realm. The Qara Khitai Gürkhan, plagued by his eastern vassals' flirtation with the Mongols and the growing power of his western rival and former vassal, the Khwarazm Shah, warmly received the Naiman prince, and gave him his daughter in marriage, hoping the refugee would enlist his kinsmen to help the declining Qara Khitai empire. Güchülüg, however, did not remain loyal to his father-in-law for long. In 1211, the year after the latter had lost his richest province, Transoxania, to the Khwarazm Shah, Güchülüg deposed the Gürkhan and usurped the Qara Khitai throne, gradually enforcing his authority throughout their former domains. Chinggis Khan's western vassals complained to their overlord about Güchülüg's oppression, and the challenge to Chinggis Khan's hegemony of such a rival power headed by a Mongol was obvious enough. In 1216 therefore Jebe led a considerable Mongol force, augmented by Uighurs and Qarluqs, against Güchülüg. Here, as in northern China, the Mongols warmly welcomed turncoats, and made full use of their familiarity with the terrain and the rival army. Güchülüg chose not to confront the Mongols on the field. Instead he ran away, aware of the divided loyalties of his troops. Jebe pursued him, finally killing him in the mountainous region of Badakhshan (in northeastern Afghanistan) in 1218.

The vacuum created by Güchülüg's death meant that the region over which he ruled (most of modern Xinjiang and Kirgizstan) became part of the emerging Mongol empire, and soon proved to be an excellent base for their next military campaigns.

The conquest of the former Qara Khitai realm was quicker and much easier than that of northern China. It was also uncharacteristically benign, mainly because the Mongols were interested in incorporating the considerable reservoir of nomadic troops formerly under Güchülüg, who were glad to replace this cruel and cowardly usurper even with Chinggis Khan. The religious factor may also have played a role in the easy conquest of the sedentary – and mostly Muslim – population. The rule of Güchülüg greatly increased the religious tension in Central Asia. Pro-Mongol Muslim sources even report that Güchülüg, a Christian who after his marriage to the Qara Khitai princess also adopted Buddhism, gave his subjects, even the many Muslims, the rather curious choice of adopting Christianity or Buddhism, or donning Khitan garb and, moreover, prohibited any public manifestation of the Islamic creed. Aware of the situation, Jebe, upon entering Kashgar, the Muslim city in which Güchülüg had taken refuge, proclaimed that everyone could adhere to his forefathers' religion. In this way he gained the population's support long before the Mongols seized Güchülüg, and was praised as the liberator of the Muslims. According to the more matter of fact Chinese version of events, however, Kashgar and its neighboring towns surrendered only after the Mongols displayed Güchülüg's head in their streets. Whatever the importance of the religious factor in the Qara Khitai conquest, the annihilation of the empire considerably enlarged the territory, manpower, wealth and prestige of Chinggis Khan. It also meant that he now ruled a significant Muslim population, and, more importantly, he now had a direct border with the strongest Muslim power in the eastern Islamic world, the empire of the Khwarazm Shah.

The relationship between the Mongols and the Khwarazm Shah began before the subjugation of the Qara Khitai realm. Aware of the rumors about the new leader of Mongolia and his victories in China, in 1215 the Khwarazm Shah sent an embassy to inquire about the new power. The ambassadors arrived at newly-conquered Zhongdu, but, strangely enough, their grisly descriptions of the looted Chinese capital did not impress the Khwarazm Shah, perhaps still intoxicated from his recent series of successful campaigns in Transoxania and Iran. Or possibly the Mongol contingents in the west had not demonstrated their military superiority in the clashes between them and the Khwarizm Shah's forces, for they were under orders to avoid fighting with the Khwarazmian army. At this point Chinggis Khan was pursuing a non-aggressive policy toward the Khwarazm Shah, his main concern being the revival of the trade routes between eastern and western Asia, which Güchülüg had tried to block. In response to the Khwarazmian embassy Chinggis therefore sent back three Muslim merchants with a message calling for peace, friendship and free movement of traders between the ruler of the East, Chinggis Khan, and the ruler of the West, Muhammad Khwarazm Shah. In the message, however, Chinggis Khan referred to the Khwarazm Shah as his dearest son, an offensive term for the haughty sultan. But after he had questioned the messengers about Chinggis Khan's force and achievements, the Khwarazm Shah appears to have accepted the pact.

The amity was shortlived, however. While the information about the early contacts between Chinggis and the Khwarazm Shah is confused and maybe fictional, all sources agree that the Utrar incident in 1218 was the event which sparked the war between the two rulers. Moreover, even the most anti-Mongol Muslim sources agree that the "bad guy" in the affair was not Chinggis Khan but Muhammad Khwarazm Shah, whose arrogant and short-sighted behavior inflicted a terrible disaster on the Muslim world. Following their agreement, Chinggis Khan sent a huge caravan of mostly Muslim merchants to Khwarazm. When the embassy arrived in Utrar, a city on Khwarazm's eastern frontier (in today's southwestern Kazakhstan), the local governor, offended by the merchants' behavior and coveting their goods, accused the merchants of spying. Obtaining the Khwarazm Shah's permission, he confiscated their goods and killed them, not knowing that "for every drop of their blood there would flow a whole Oxus." (Juwaynī, 1997: 80). When the enraged Chinggis Khan heard about the massacre, he was still calm enough to suggest a diplomatic solution, demanding that the Khwarazm Shah execute the governor of Utrar and return the caravan's goods to restore peace between the two realms. The Khwarazm Shah killed one of the three envoys Chinggis Khan had sent him, thereby breaching the norm of the ambassadors' "diplomatic immunity." The other two he sent back, not before shaving their beards to humiliate them as well as the one who had dispatched them. This meant war.

Later Muslim sources sometimes blamed the Abbasid Caliph, alleging that, annoyed by Khwarazm Shah's attack on his legitimacy and by the abortive Khwarazmian campaign in Iraq in 1217, he had urged Chinggis Khan to invade the Muslim world. This view, probably originating in Khwarazmian propaganda and later embellished with details such as the caliph sending a regiment of Franks to Chinggis Khan for operations against Khwarazm, seems to be groundless. The Utrar incident was certainly a sufficient *casus belli*.

Chinggis Khan did not set out for the west before carefully preparing what was about to be by far his largest and logistically most complicated campaign. The preparations included appointing a successor. Chinggis Khan was already nearly sixty years old, he was about to go on a dangerous mission, and, as one of his wives pointed out, it made sense to secure his realm by avoiding the most common danger for a nomadic empire: a struggle over succession. The selected heir, Chinggis Khan's third son, Ögödei, was chosen because of his generosity and affable character which gave him the best chance of keeping the family together. Whether Chinggis Khan meant permanently to entrust Mongol leadership to the Ögödeid branch of the family was an issue fiercely (and sometimes bloodily) contested in Mongol and post-Mongol politics for centuries.

But most of Chinggis's preparations were military rather than political: he collected troops and specialists from his subjects, including, most importantly, northern Chinese siege engineers. The Tanguts refused to send auxiliaries westward, maybe because their troops were already assisting Mongol operation against the Jin, but the Mongol army included northern Chinese, Khitans, Uighurs, Qarluqs, and troops from the Tarim Basin population previously under Güchülüg's rule. Many of the soldiers were familiar with the terrain and the enemy, since Transoxania and Khwarazm as well as many of Chinggis Khan's western vassals had formerly been under Qara Khitai rule. The Mongols thus had good intelligence. The force also had quite a significant Muslim segment. In 1219 this composite Mongol army advanced to Utrar, the root of the conflict. There, Chinggis divided his troops: two sons, Ögödei and Chaghadai, stayed to besiege Utrar; Jochi, the eldest son, was sent down the Jaxartes river, heading for Khwarazm, while Chinggis Khan, his youngest son Tolui and the main Mongol army advanced toward Bukhara. Even more than in North China, the ability of the different Mongol columns to act separately and then rejoin and act together or start a new mission was a major feature of the Mongol campaign in the Muslim world.

Though his army was numerically by far superior to the Mongol force, the Khwarazm Shah did not try to confront the Mongols in the field. Instead, perhaps afraid of his own soldiers no less than of the Mongols, Muhammad Khwarazm Shah divided his troops into garrisons at his principal towns and improved their fortifications. The descriptions of Sultan Muhammad rebuilding Samarqand's walls while muttering to himself: "what am I doing, it's futile to confront the Mongols anyway" are anachronistic, but there is no doubt that the defensive strategy he chose was ill conceived and probably would not have served him well even if it had been executed with greater vigor.

After five months of siege the Mongols entered Utrar, putting the whole populace to the sword in retribution for the caravan incident. Utrar's citadel and walls were leveled to the ground and its ruler was brought alive to Chinggis Khan who personally supervised his execution. While Utrar was besieged, Chinggis Khan advanced toward

Bukhara, a major commercial and religious center of Transoxania which was less heavily fortified than Samarqand, the Khwarazmian capital. Instead of taking the usual route to Bukhara, via Samarqand, Chinggis Khan, with the guidance of a local defector, chose to cross the allegedly impenetrable Kizil Kom (red sands) desert (see map 3). The appearance of the Mongol force in early 1220 before Bukhara's gates, some 650 km behind the enemy line, was therefore totally unexpected. The stunned Khwarazmian garrison turned to flight, but was overtaken by the Mongols and slaughtered to a man. The startled population, led by its religious officials, opened the city gates to the Mongols. A few hundred soldiers, however, remained in Bukhara's citadel, from which they offered strong resistance to the Mongols for twelve days before being overwhelmed and killed. The fate of Bukhara can be seen as a model of Mongol treatment of the Transoxanian cities: the people were herded out of the town so that it could be looted without interruption. Useful people – mainly artisans, especially weapon makers and weavers – were selected for transportation eastward to work for the Mongols. Young men were taken to serve as arrow fodder in the Mongols' next battle, and young women were taken for the pleasure of the invading troops. In addition, Chinggis Khan demanded compensation, equal to the value of the goods taken from his merchants in Utrar, from the city's notables and wealthy traders. While the city was sacked, a fire broke out, reducing the wooden houses to ashes. Juwayni depicts Chinggis Khan as addressing the Bukharans from their Friday mosque (which, mistaking it for the Shah's palace, he had turned into a stable), and claiming "I'm the punishment of God! If you had not committed great sins he would have not sent a punishment like me" (Juwayni 1997: 105). This may well be anachronistic, but no doubt the rumors about the coming of an unknown bewildering enemy began to spread rapidly.

From Bukhara, Chinggis Khan turned toward the Khwarazmian capital, Samarqand, arriving with a sizable host of Bukharan citizens who created the impression of a huge army. A significant segment of the Khwarazmian troops, who had already chosen to switch sides, also joined him, as did Ögödei and Chaghadai after the fall of Utrar. When Chinggis learned that the Khwarazm Shah had already fled westward, he sent two of his finest generals, Jebe and Sübetei, to pursue him, while he himself attacked the capital. Samarqand was heavily fortified, guarded by a huge garrison of the Khwarazmian elite troops strengthened by elephants, but it took only a few days of siege to convince the city's religious authorities to open the gates for the Mongols. The Mongols did not harm them but they systematically destroyed the city walls, creating "free passage to horse and foot." Then they drove out the population, apart from those who received the protection of the religious leaders, and plundered the city. The citadel garrison that continued to fight after the city surrendered was slain and the citadel ruined. 30,000 artisans were sent to Mongolia, together with beautiful women; "arrow fodder" was also collected for the continuation of the campaign. Chinggis Khan appointed governors, and the remains of the population were allowed to buy their right to enter the city. With the conquest of Samarqand (May–June 1220), nearly all of Transoxania was in Mongol hands less than a year after the Mongols crossed the Jaxartes. Chinggis retreated to the steppe south of the city, resting his army and horses for the summer.

In the meantime Jochi was advancing through the lower Jaxartes region toward Khwarazm, the homeland of Sultan Muhammad. With the assistance of his brothers, who joined him after Samarqand submitted, he defeated the renowned Khwarazmian commanders in 1221, and reduced Urgench, the surviving capital of Khwarazm, into an "abode of jackals and the haunt of owl and kite." The Mongols took the town, destroying the buildings and slaughtering its inhabitants. After the remains of the population had been driven out of the city and divided according to their skills, the *coup de grace* was the opening of the Oxus dikes. The city was flooded, its remaining buildings collapsed and even the few who had found good hiding places were flushed out. Jochi and Chaghadai then continued northward, defeating the nearby Qipchaq tribes, traditionally Khwarazm's allies, one after another.

Simultaneously Jebe and Sübetei were sweeping across northwestern Iran in pursuit of the Khwarazm Shah. They advanced throughout Iran, raiding the countryside and receiving the submission of many terrified cities, and reached the borders of Iraq, where the horrified Caliph began to recruit a united Muslim front against them. When they found out that the Khwarazm Shah had gone to Azerbaijan, however, they turned northward, postponing the conflict with the Caliph for a few decades. Incapable of anything but flight, the desperate Khwarazm Shah finally found refuge on a small island in the Caspian Sea where, in late 1220 or early 1221, Jebe and Sübetei heard about his death (of either heart break or pneumonia). This "second Alexander" ended his life lonesome and destitute, buried in the rotten shirt of the only slave still serving him.

His pursuers, however, returned home the long way round: they continued through Azerbaijan into the Caucasus and up to the Crimea, defeating the local people and tribes (Georgians, Alans, Qipchaqs and Circassians), and galloping across the Russian steppe, where in May 1223 they crushed a coalition of Qipchaq tribes and Russian princes in the battle of the Khalka river, near the Azov Sea. The conquest of Russia however was left to Chinggis's heir: following this great raid, Jebe and Sübetei retreated from the Russian steppe, the Caucasus and Azerbaijan without leaving garrisons or governors, to rejoin Chinggis Khan's troops on their way back to Mongolia.

Before Chinggis went back, however, he had to make sure that no opposition would remain in the former Khwarizmian realm. For this reason he sent Tolui to Khurasan, the large and important Khwarazmian province south of the Oxus, the fortified cities of which challenged the Mongol troops. Chinggis soon found himself involved in pursuing Jalal al-Din Khwarazm Shah, Muhammad's son and eventual heir, and the only Muslim leader to offer effective opposition to the Mongols at this time. After his father's death, Jalal al-Din made for Ghazna (in modern Afghanistan), his former appanage, and managed to rally a considerable following, composed of local people and remnants of the Khwarazmian troops. With their help he managed twice to inflict defeats upon small Mongol contingents, the only setbacks they suffered during their western campaign. These provoked Chinggis to come to defeat Jalal al-Din in person. The two finally met in November 1221 on the banks of the Indus river. The warrior qualities of Jalal al-Din won the admiration of Chinggis but this did not enable him to win the battle: deserted by half of his troops, and watching the other half being slain by the Mongols, Jalal al-Din barely escaped by riding into the river and crossing into India. With the shattering of Jalal al-Din's force, the war in the west was practically over, though Tolui continued to fight in Khurasan till 1223, as did

Jebe and Subetei further northward. The chase after Jalal al-Din, first into India and then to Azerbaijan, continued till his death in 1231, thereby keeping a Mongol presence in the Muslim lands west of Transoxania even after Chinggis Khan turned back to Mongolia.

Before attacking, Mongol forces always sent messengers calling on populations and polities to submit and destroy their fortifications. The Mongols proclaimed that they would do no harm to those who surrendered peacefully, but would not leave alive anybody who resisted them, a dire threat which worked well especially after stories about the fate of Transoxania began to spread. One must bear in mind, however, that even cities that submitted peaceably were harshly treated. Some were indeed spared of plunder and slaughter but the Mongols always demanded manpower and taxes for their continuing conquest, sometimes several times a year. This explains why so many cities rebelled against the Mongols, especially when the rumors of Jalal al-Din's victories began to circulate. Rebellious towns, however, were treated without mercy, and Tolui's march through Khurasan was therefore extremely brutal. Moreover, revenge was still a major issue for the Mongols and therefore most unfortunate were the places where a Chinggisid was killed in battle: none of the citizens of Bamyan, in Afghanistan, survived after Chinggis's beloved grandson fell during the fighting for the city (though unlike the Taliban in March 2001 the Mongols kept the great Buddha sculptures of the town intact). In Nishapur, a major city in Khurasan whose populace was guilty not only of rebellion but also of killing a son-in-law of Chinggis Khan, Tolui and his widowed sister first exterminated the whole population (including cats and dogs) and then yoked oxen and ploughed over the city.

The sources recall a few acts of personal courage among the fighting Muslims, but there are many more stories of panic, including that of a single Mongol soldier who captured a hundred Muslims; even with these favorable odds none of the Muslims dared resist, all waiting patiently in line while the Mongol beheaded one after another. The speed, efficiency and disdain for human life which accompanied the conquest can certainly account for this kind of panic. The hasty disintegration of the Khwarazm empire, however, resulted also from the internal weakness of this newly fashioned polity, whose subjects and troops lacked cohesion or loyalty.

Moreover, since the Khwarazm Shah had annihilated most of the local elites in the regions he conquered, there were few leaders, apart from his son, who could offer more than local resistance to the Mongols.

After resting his troops from the pursuit after Jalal al-Din, Chinggis considered going back to Mongolia through India, but the climate and terrain convinced him to turn back north. A bad omen sealed his decision: in the Afghan mountains the Mongols encountered a rhinoceros. The appearance of the unknown beast, understood as the mythical unicorn, was explained by Chinggis's astrologer as an immediate order to leave the Indian route and return home through Transoxania. More practical reason for the quick march northward was the news on the rebellion of the Tanguts, who in 1223 withdrew their troops from the Mongol force deployed against the Jin.

The war against the Tanguts was Chinggis's final campaign. In the spring of 1225, when he finally returned to Mongolia, leaving only governors and small garrisons in the west, he offered the rebellious Tangut monarch an opportunity to signal his submission by sending his son as a hostage to the Mongol court. The latter declined and in 1225 he went so far as to sign a peace treaty with the Jin. In spring 1226 the Mongols appeared on the Tangut western border, and in several coordinated columns subdued the Xi Xia urban centers one after another. By early 1227 they besieged the Tangut capital, the last stronghold of the Xi Xia. Shortly before its final collapse, in August 1227, Chinggis Khan fell ill and died, apparently from the complications of a riding accident he had suffered nearly two years beforehand. (Or, more colorfully, his heart was said to have weakened after he had seen the white-as-milk blood of the injured Tangut ruler; or he was mortally injured during intercourse with his Tangut concubine, who wished to avenge her kin). According to his orders, the Tangut campaign was continued, and their capital fell in September, without the enemy knowing that the Mongol leader was dead. Either because this was Chinggis Khan's last wish or because the Mongols wanted to assuage their pain on their leader's death, the Tanguts were treated with extreme ferocity; their capital was turned into dust and its population was eradicated. According to Mongol custom, Chinggis Khan was buried in a secret place high in the mountains. Legend says that soon after his body was put to rest a huge tree rose and covered the grave and that all the rank and file who had participated in his funeral were killed, so they would not be able to reveal the tomb's location. The secret was indeed well kept, and the search for Chinngis Khan's grave has continued ever since, attracting archaeologists, adventurers and politicians from around the globe to this day.

* * *

In the transformation of Chinggis Khan from a successful chieftain to world conqueror, the invasion of the Muslim world was a turning point. This was not only because it significantly enlarged the territory under his possession, adding the lands of modern Uzbekistan, Tajikistan, Afghanistan and parts of Kazakhstan and Turkmenistan (while raids conducted by his army also crossed Iran, the Caucasus and parts of Russia) or the amount of people and riches at his disposal. The speedy annihilation of the Khwarazm Shah's power also enhanced his prestige and bolstered his public image as someone pre-destined by Heaven to conquer the entire world. Moreover, this invasion also closely exposed him to a sedentary culture different from that of China, the major reference point of Mongolian nomads throughout history. Unlike his predecessors Chinggis Khan could now learn "the laws and the customs of the cities" not only from China but also from the Muslim world; the stock of administrative, military and cultural tools he appropriated was therefore larger and more diverse than those of former nomadic empires. Chinggis was no longer following the Liao or Jin model, he was launching one of his own, and the creative use the Mongols found for the diverse traditions of their subjects was soon to become one of the main hallmarks of their multi-cultural empire.

Owen Lattimore has pointed out another strategic advantage of the invasion which also served to distinguish Chinggis's experience from that of the Liao and Jin: by turning from North China to Turkestan, Chinggis Khan was avoiding the classical mistake of previous steppe rulers, namely to leave the steppe unsubdued when they established themselves in northern China, with the result that they were sooner or later overthrown by a fresh nomadic force from the steppe. By incorporating the steppe people of both the eastern and western steppes under his authority, as he did by conquering Central Asia, Chinggis Khan secured his rear and enabled his heirs to continue with the conquest of the sedentary regions without being threatened by a newly established nomadic force (Lattimore 1963: 6–7; cited in Morgan 1986: 73). Nothing suggests that, when Chinggis Khan turned toward Khwarazm, he had such a grand design in mind, but the near monopoly on steppe warriors he achieved following his Central Asian campaign greatly facilitated further expansion.

Moreover, it was during the Central Asian campaign, partly due to the vacuum established after the demise of the Khwarazm Shah (and Güchülüg before him), that conquest became a strategy, not a tactic. Chinggis Khan found himself ruling over vast territories and began to turn them into an empire.

FOUNDATIONS OF AN EMPIRE

Going over Muslim descriptions of the Mongol invasion, a never-ending scene of bloodbaths and devastation, it is tempting to adopt their point of view and to treat the Mongols like an apocalyptic whirlwind of destruction, descending from nowhere and leaving swathes of wasteland behind. This, however, is far from the truth. There was a method in the madness, both strategically and politically.

Even though the numbers of victims mentioned in the chronicles are greatly inflated – no medieval Muslim city contained the 2.4 million people which, according to Juzjani, was the number of people murdered at Herat – certainly the destruction and loss of life which accompanied the Mongol onslaught were on an unparalleled scale. And yet the Mongols hardly indulged in wanton cruelty for its own sake; the destruction and massacres served Mongol strategic considerations, not their sadistic needs. This strategy derived mainly from demographic considerations: the Mongols were always outnumbered by their subjects and rivals. Butchering whole cities was one way by which the Mongols tried – cruelly but effectively – to deal with this demographic imbalance. Moreover, the mass killing was also a very effective psychological weapon: if one city was massacred, the next city was more likely to surrender without further resistance, thus avoiding unnecessary Mongol casualties. The devastation had psychological value as well as serving tactical needs: despite their improved technical ability and equipment, storming fortified towns was always a time-consuming and costly undertaking. By reducing walls and fortresses to ashes, the Mongols ensured that they would not have to deal again with such fortifications, and this policy also facilitated the further movement of nomadic troops in the region. Moreover, the devastation and depopulation were meant to limit future resistance, both by the panic they created and because the Mongols ravaged much more territory than they kept: Chinggis Khan left governors in Transoxania but his troops devastated Khurasan, Iran, Azerbaijan and the Caucasus. By acting in this fashion, like a tsunami or tidal wave, as Timothy May described it, raiding and wrecking havoc over a vast territory and then consolidating their authority in only part of it, the Mongols created a broad belt of destruction around their borders. This belt protected their territory from future opposition, facilitated their continuous expansion, and created pasture lands. Motivated by the wars' practical demands, by their blind obedience to Chinggis Khan and his generals and by their firm belief that they were implementing the will of Heaven, combined with a certain nomadic disdain toward sedentary people "who eat grass like beasts," often supplemented by the desire to seek revenge, the Mongols were able to practice mass killing and destruction without remorse.

Moreover, the incredible amount of destruction had a considerable impact on the shaping of the governance in the emerging empire. While the Mongols' steppe predecessors practiced mainly indirect rule, preserving most of the former order and leadership in their subject territories, the Mongols, whose violent conquest often eliminated local rulers and elites alike, of necessity created a more direct mode of government. The Mongols were justly suspicious of the local population, whose willingness to cooperate with the conquerors was certainly hampered by the brutality of the conquest, so they preferred to limit the use of locals in their administration and to rely mainly on imported foreign specialists.

The Mongols' pragmatic cruelty came as a shock to the Muslim world, not least because it was so different from the behavior of earlier steppe conquerors they had known: even though some of their invasions did include killing, looting, and destroying, the Turks arrived gradually, in relatively small groups and after going through a process of acculturation, which often included Islamization and prepared them for a symbiotic relationship with their sedentary subjects. The Mongols, however, came with tremendous speed and without acculturation. Moreover, they imported to the region the cruel methods of East-Asian warfare. Chinese and Mongol sources (the *Secret History*) are much more prosaic than Muslim and later European sources in their descriptions of the Mongol invasion: even the grisly descriptions of the Jin capital, Zhongdu, derive from Muslim and not from Chinese witnesses. Descriptions of pre-Mongol warfare in China routinely include features such as elimination of the non-combatant populations during internal conflicts, and during the Jin-Song war of 1206–8 we hear of prisoners' heads being hurled by the dozens into a besieged town with catapults, suggesting that war in the Chinese vicinity tended to be bloodier, more cruel and marked by a more thoroughgoing indifference to human life than in the Muslim east at that time. This may partially account for both the behaviour of the Mongols and for the Muslim shock.

All this being said, however, one should bear in mind that the destruc- tion and depopulation caused by the Mongols were neither permanent nor were they irreversible.[1] Again it is easy to buy into the gloomy, apocalyptic narrative of the Muslim sources, which suggest that a thousand years will not be enough to repair the damage done by the Mongols. This, however, is quite misleading. True, the devastation was not uniform and some regions, especially those within the outer band of destruction and later on those located on the frontiers between rival khanates, revived very slowly or never achieved their former glory. Yet in parts of the Mongol empire, e.g. Transoxania, the revival was nearly as fast as the ruination, and the Mongols were responsible for this as well, though less directly than for the initial destruction. This is because during his stay in Central Asia Chinggis Khan was not only carefully coordinating the movements of his forces, but also laying the institutional foundations for his empire.

Several policies were apparent already in the 1220s, and they reflect a central planning that gradually rises above the day-to-day demands of warfare. Throughout the battles, for example, artisans were registered,

[1] This was first pointed out by Bernard Lewis in 1968, although he turned attention mainly to parts of the Muslim world which were not harmed by the Mongols. I argue that even major parts that were harmed were quickly restored.

transported and relocated to Mongolia, northern China or Uighuristan, to meet the needs of the empire – from weapons to gilded brocade – while East Asian craftsmen, physicians and farmers were transferred westward when required. The routes and bridges from East to West Asia were constantly repaired and broadened to allow the fast traffic of troops, edicts, envoys and goods. Trade was much encouraged by the Mongols, not only by creating the required infrastructure of travel but also because, made suddenly wealthy with newly acquired booty, they were both enthusiastic consumers of and major investors in international commerce. Already by 1221, as military operations in Central Asia were reaching a climax, an active commerce in luxury goods had already developed within the Mongol empire, comprising Mongolia, northern China, Uighuria, Khurasan and the Hindu Kush mountains. In Mongolia itself bulk goods like flour were also sold at an elevated price, since the traders, many of them Muslims, were quick to exploit the free-spending attitudes of the nouveau-riche Mongols. The Mongols also soon recognized the need to communicate with subjects in their native languages and a host of secretaries recorded Chinggis's edicts in Chinese, Uighur and Persian.

Simultaneously Chinggis Khan was also laying the basis for a local administration, appointing commissioners or *darughachis* (literally, "those who press the seal") in the regions in which the Mongols intended to stay. At this point the commissioners held both civil and military authority. Their mission was to ensure that the town, region, or social group under their sway would remain under Mongol rule and provide the empire with what it needed in the form of taxes or manpower. The other part of their responsibility was, therefore, to help these places return to normalcy. The people chosen for these posts were men "familiar with the customs and laws of the cities," who had already proven their loyalty to the Mongols. In fact the appointment was often a reward for a special service: the first *darughachi* in northern China, appointed in 1215, for instance, was Ja'far Khwaja, the merchant who guided the Mongols through the mountain passes into northern China. The Mongols' commissioners came from a variety of ethnic and religious backgrounds, but they were literate, multilingual, and with earlier experience either as traders or in the bureaucracy of former post-nomadic empires (mainly Khitans, Uighurs,

Khwarazmians). Many of them were assigned to regions far from their original home. Thus Chinggis Khan (or his son) sent the Khwarazmian trader Mahmud Yalawach to rule in northern China while the Khitan Yelü Ahai came to govern Transoxania, presiding over a multi-ethnic staff, which included many Chinese. At least in the case of Transoxania we have good evidence that already in 1222 and certainly in 1224–5 life there was already springing back to normal. Chang Chun, the Daoist patriarch summoned by Chinggis Khan who spent 1222–23 in Transoxania, is often quoted as saying that after the Mongol onslaught Samarqand's population was reduced to one quarter of its original 100,000 households. Less attention has been given to his evidence of the thriving markets, and the flourishing agriculture of Samarqand where grain, vegetables and fruits (including the famous melons which captivated every traveler to the region throughout the ages) were abundant. While the echoes of the war are still felt in the account of Chang Chun, the travelogue of Yelü Chucai, the Khitan advisor and astrologer of Chinggis Khan who accompanied him in his western campaign and remained in Central Asia several months after him, till late 1225, is even more impressive. Chucai described Samarqand as a heavenly place, dedicating many poems to its beautiful gardens. The city had "a very wealthy and dense population" with striving monetary commerce, and exceptional agricultural products. Bukhara, he added, was even richer than Samarqand, and Urgench, the newly rebuilt Khwarazm capital, was richer than both. The agricultural revival, attested by the two Chinese travelers, is especially worth noting, since the depopulation and the neglect of irrigation work during the Mongol invasion were often described as resulting in an enduring damage to agricultural production. The Chinese, Khitan and Tangut farmers Chang Chun met near Samarqand probably bore some of the responsibility for the quick recovery of Transoxanian agriculture. Muslim biographical sources also attest that when Mongol governors began functioning, people who had sought refuge in the mountains or elsewhere gradually returned to the city and to their fields.

The undisturbed profession of Muslim religious life, also attested by Chang Chun, despite the unbelief of both rulers and governors, must have also contributed to the quick revival. There was nothing anti-Islamic in Chinggis Khan's campaign against Khwarazm, and indeed his "religious tolerance" is one of the few features of his career that have always been deemed positive by outside observers. The Mongols emerged in a multi-religious environment in which no religion was considered exclusive. Chinggis Khan certainly held holy men of all faiths in high esteem. Those who impressed him, like the Daoist priest Chang Chun he summoned to Central Asia to reveal to him the secret of longevity, or the Buddhist patriarch Hai Yun his generals had encountered in North China, received tax exemptions and other privileges. In return they were supposed to pray for the Khan's wellbeing.[2] Devoid of any missionary zeal, Chinggis Khan was ready to let everybody adhere to his own faith, as long as the customs of the different religions did not conflict with Mongol customs and as long as the religions displayed no threat to his political position. If it did pose a threat, as in the case of the shaman Teb Tengri, no ecumenical considerations limited his actions. Nor did the Mongols hesitate cynically to use religion for tactical needs: when Jebe and Sübetei arrived at Armenia, for example, they put the sign of the cross over their soldiers' shields, to convince the Christian Armenians to refrain from fighting their co-religionists. When the latter relaxed after seeing the cross, Jebe and Sübetei attacked them. The Mongols were also quick to acknowledge the benefit of winning people's acquiescence through their religious leaders and through freedom of worship. Their religious tolerance was therefore part of their practice of *Realpolitik*. meant not only to secure them, in the words of David Morgan, maximum celestial insurance (Morgan 1986: 44), but also, perhaps mainly, to facilitate their rule in the subjugated lands.

Another of Chinggis's actions was to assign appanages to his family members. Most famous (and disputed centuries after his death) were

---

[2] No Muslim holy men, however, impressed the Khan like Chang Chun or Hai Yun. The closest example is that of the Herati *qadi* Wahid al-Din. Falling off unharmed from the walls of Herat, he was considered by the Mongol troops to be blessed. They brought him to Chinggis Khan, who asked him whether the Muslim scriptures predicted his rise to power. The *qadi* cited apocalyptic traditions on the coming of the Turks, and the Great Khan was highly pleased. The *qadi*, however, lost the Khan's favor after he had pointed out that if Chinggis continued to massacre the population, nobody would be left to commemorate his fame.

the appanages he allocated to his four major sons. Jochi, the eldest, was the first to receive his territorial basis in the Irtish valley, and this territory was later to be extended to the northwest "as far as the hoofs of the Tatar horse had penetrated." The other family members got their territories later, probably during the early 1220s. Chaghadai received the land between Uighuria and the Oxus, roughly the former Qara Khitai territory; Ögödei got Zungaria (in northern Xinjiang) and the western slopes of the Altai, a small territory since as the future Great Khan he was going to receive plenty of lands *ex officio*; and the appanage of Tolui, the youngest, was in the fatherland, Mongolia. In fact the assignments were more numerous and complicated, including allocation of territory and people to Chinggis's brothers, wives, daughters, and other kin. The reasoning behind these allocations was double: first, in continuation of the Turco-Mongol tradition, the empire was regarded as a jointly owned property, a common pool of wealth meant to benefit the whole Chinggisid family. Second, assigning each prince a wide area for the grazing of his herds was meant to avoid conflict. The outcome, however, was nearly the opposite, as local and central interests were often at odds. Already in Chinggis's lifetime, Jochi's identification with his own territory gave rise to rumors that he had tried to ally himself with the Muslims (of Khwarazm) against his father, a policy which might have led Chinggis to engineer his death, which occurred about six months before his own. The tension between the collegial character of the empire and its central government remained a feature of the Mongol empire after Chinggis's death.

THE SUCCESS: WHY DID SUCH CONQUESTS NEVER HAPPEN BEFORE?

The circumstances at the time of Chinggis Khan's rise to power, above all the political divisions in Mongolia and Asia and the ripening of a post-nomadic tradition in the Eurasian steppe, certainly contributed to his success, as discussed in chapters one and two. But the actions Chinggis Khan took himself account for the major part of his unparalleled achievements. We can start with his military machine.

The Army

The Mongols did not succeed due to a technological breakthrough or magic weapon: in terms of armament and tactics they basically continued the traditional form of steppe warfare.[3] What made them superior to other steppe armies was their better organization and strategic planning.

As seen in chapter two, the Mongol army was not organized according to tribal lines. Its generals were therefore chosen not on the basis of descent or status but rather according to their military talents, proven in the wars in Mongolia, and their personal loyalty to Chinggis. The quality of leadership in the Mongol army was therefore much higher than in former nomadic troops, and Chinggis could rely completely on a brilliant group of generals, assigning to them tasks in different and distant fronts, and thereby enabling the Mongols both to conduct complex coordinated operations and to campaign simultaneously in different parts of Asia.

Another distinguishing feature of the Mongol army was its strict discipline. This was maintained by fostering the loyalty of the troops to their generals, who became their new "chiefs", and above them, to Chinggis, as well as by draconian measures; anyone found plundering without permission was put to death as was anyone who abandoned his unit or fled the field. The key idea behind these draconian measures was that the warriors must act as a unit and not according to their individual aspirations. Collective training, mostly in the form of great hunts (practiced also by earlier nomadic warriors) also strengthened this notion. The strict discipline was essential for coordinated operations, which characterized so many Mongol campaigns.

The decimal organization of the army was also a useful mechanism for incorporating former rivals or subject troops, in that it made it possible to disperse them among different units. This efficient incorporation meant that the more the Mongols conquered, the more manpower they had for their next conquests.

[3] Recently the role of gunpowder weapons was mentioned as one reason for Chinggis Khan's success. Yet while Chinese and Mongols certainly used incendiary projectiles and the Mongols may have played a leading role in introducing gunpowder to the Muslim world and to Europe, there is no decisive evidence for the use of firearms or cannon in the battles fought by Chinggis and his immediate heirs.

Mongol campaigns were thoroughly planned. The planning included obtaining information about the enemy and his terrain from traders, subjects and turncoats, and also during the campaign through the use of scouts advancing some 50 km ahead of the main force. The planning also included the assignment of specific missions, routes and pasture lands to generals who headed individual columns, and the fixing of timetables and meeting points in which the columns were to meet during the campaign. Another facet of the central planning was the procurement of weapons, first by collecting and distributing the plundered enemy's weaponry and later by distributing those produced by conscripted artisans' colonies for their Mongol masters. The armament of the Mongols also improved as their conquests continued.

In the field, the Mongols made maximum use of the mobility of their light mounted archers, using classical steppe methods such as hit-and-run tactics accompanied by showers of arrows, surprise attacks, encircling maneuvers, ambushes and feigned retreat. They preferred first to disperse the enemy's field armies, ravage the countryside and small towns, and to take the main stronghold (e.g., Zhongdu, Samarqand, the Xi Xia capital) only after its population had been physically and psychologically exhausted. The Mongols were masters of psychological warfare, often meant to conceal their numerical inferiority, and they did not hesitate to use deceit and subterfuge. The most successful psychological warfare, which was also a strategic asset, as described above, was the unparalleled use of massacre and devastation. The tsunami strategy applied in the Khwarazm war was essential for Mongol success. Finally, the Mongols targeted leaders, hunting them down and eliminating them, thereby securing the submission of their troops. In this way, Chinggis Khan created a formidable military machine which managed to mobilize military resources more efficiently than earlier nomads, and, moreover, the more the Mongols conquered, the more resources they accumulated for future expansion.

The Willingness to Learn from Others

Another major reason for Chinggis's and his heirs' success was their willingness to learn from foreigners – subjects, neighbors, and visitors

– and their skill in doing so. This was apparent in the military field, where the Mongols appropriated much of the military knowledge of both China and the Muslim world in forming their own units of siege engineers, and established workshops for weapon manufacturing manned by their subjects. After Chinggis's time, they even built a navy: quite an achievement for people who originated so far from the sea. Yet the military part was only one facet of a more comprehensive Mongol policy: Chinggis was quick to realize that consolidating an empire required new skills that the Mongols lacked, and he either adopted these – as he did with the Uighur alphabet as early as 1204 – or employed specialists who possessed such knowledge. Nomadic culture creates generalists, and every nomad is versed in a variety of skills that allow him to survive in the steppe, but these are not enough for ruling a world empire. The Mongols therefore looked for specialists of all kinds, whether in the domain of religion, military technology, weaving, astronomy, or medicine and the like, and redistributed them across their empire. The manning of Mongol administration by such specialists in Chinggis's time is another manifestation of their resourceful use of the talents of their subjects.

Political and Diplomatic Skills

As he proved already during the unification of Mongolia, Chinggis Khan was not only a great military leader and an extremely open-minded man, he was also a unique political leader. Thus, for example, he skillfully exploited ethnic, dynastic and religious conflicts among his rivals; he used two influential groups, religious men and traders, to gain support among his subjects; he had an eye for talented people whom he promoted regardless of their descent or former status; and he understood the importance of appointing an heir for securing the smooth transition of power after his death. Moreover, he chose well: his successor, Ögödei, proved himself highly capable not only in the field but also in governance, developing many of his father's ad hoc decisions into a systematic policy in the fields of administration, religion and law.

SUCCESS

But beyond the favorable context, his unique military and political leadership and his open-minded approach to new knowledge and skills, a major factor in the overwhelming success of Chinggis Khan was success itself. His career seems to prove the cliché that nothing succeeds like success. Every victory he gained further stimulated his soldiers to continue fighting for him and encouraged rivals to submit without a fight. In this respect fate and fortune also played a role in his success: Chinggis never suffered a humiliating defeat; his later victories were easier and quicker than his first attempts in China – nothing stained his unmatched record. Therefore, every additional victory also bolstered his public image as a person pre-ordained by heaven to conquer the world, a mission which under his heirs became the collective destiny of the Mongols. Initially Chinggis aspired only to rule over the Mongol *ulus*, the felt-tents dwellers, or the nomadic world centered in Mongolia. The broadening of the horizons occurred gradually, due to the flight of rivals to neighboring empires (the Tanguts and the Qara Khitai) and through the increased presence of literati of Chinese and Khitan origin among his advisers, for whom ruling all-under-heaven was the natural ideology of a ruler. More than anything else, it was his unprecedented success against the Khwarazm Shah which convinced Chinggis – as well as his contemporaries – that he owned the *qut* or *suu*, the charisma and divine grace. His career was therefore pre-ordained, and whoever opposed him, also opposed the will of heaven, which meant that he was doomed to failure and had to be subdued. Moreover, his overwhelming success also convinced Chinggis that the mandate he had received was wider than those of his nomadic predecessors, in that it encompassed the whole world, with both its nomadic and its sedentary realms. This is evident from the will Chinggis Khan left to his sons: to subjugate every place which dared to oppose the Mongols.

Chinggis Khan's invasion into the Muslim world was a turning point in his road into world conquest. It also proved a turning point in the history of the Muslim world, as will be discussed in the next chapter.

THE CHINGGISID LEGACY IN
THE MUSLIM WORLD

They came, they sapped, they burnt, they slew, they plundered and they departed.

Juwayni [twice!!] 1997: 107.

In these days when, thank God, all corners of the earth are under our control and that of Chinggis Khan's illustrious family, and philosophers, astronomers, scholars and historians of all religions and nations – Cathay, Machin, India, Kashmir, Tibet, Uyghur and other nations of the Turks, Arabs and Franks – are gathered in droves at our glorious court, each and every one of them possesses copies of the histories, stories and beliefs of their own people, and they are well informed of some of them.

Rashid/Thackson 1998–9: 1: 6 (Ghazan Khan commissioning the
writing of *Jami' al-tawarikh* by Rashid al-Din)

And the sun of the creed of Muhammad casts its shadow over countries whose nostrils had not been perfumed by the scent of Islam … whereas today so many believers in the one God have bent their steps thitherwards and reached the farthest countries of the East and settled and made their homes there, that their numbers are beyond calculation or computation.

Juwayni/Boyle 1997: 13

One of the common popular ideas about the impact of Chinggis Khan and his heirs in the Muslim world is that they left no legacy beyond destruction. After about a century (with the fall of the Mongol state in Iran in 1335), they simply vanished from the Muslim stage leaving nothing positive behind, having caused disastrous destruction that would take centuries to repair. The negativity of this legacy is often stressed by Muslim authors in the comparison of the Mongol invasions and the Arab conquests of the seventh to eighth centuries: the conquests of Islam, almost devoid of massive massacres and destruction, were more gradual, and encompassed less territory. However, they resulted in the rise of an enduring civilization distinguished in its religion, language and script, while those of Chinggis Khan were allegedly ephemeral, resulting only in devastation and decline.

The historical picture, however, is much more complex. First, as will be demonstrated in the first part of this chapter, the Mongols did not disappear from the Muslim world in the fourteenth century. In fact, descendants of Chinggis Khan ruled in the western steppe, Muslim Central Asia, and India until the eighteenth and nineteenth centuries. Second, while the Mongols never created a civilization comparable to the Muslim one, Mongol rule left a rich and enduring legacy in the Muslim world and beyond. The nature of this legacy, however, makes it easy to ignore or denigrate it, since what the Mongols left behind was not their ethnic culture but their decidedly different imperial culture. Thus Chinggis Khan neither preached a new religion nor tried to disseminate his shamanic beliefs; instead his descendants eventually embraced one of the universal religions represented by a certain group of their subjects. Nor did Chinggis Khan promote Mongolian as this empire's *lingua franca*. The Mongol empire remained multilingual, and, in the Muslim world, the Mongols began to replace Mongolian with Turkish as early as the thirteenth century. Yet Mongol imperial culture – comprising not only the Mongols' own social and cultural norms but also the indigenous traditions and institutions of the conquered people and of the foreign traditions imported by the Chinggisids – left its enduring mark on the Muslim world. This, as will be explained in the remainder of this chapter, was mainly in terms of broadening Muslim horizons through intensive cross-cultural contacts, the further expansion of Islam, ethnic and geo-political changes, and political culture.

HISTORICAL OVERVIEW: THE ENDURANCE OF THE CHINGGISIDS IN THE MUSLIM WORLD

The Mongol expansion into the Muslim world and elsewhere continued throughout the period of the united Mongol empire (1206–1260), leading to the creation of the greatest continuous land empire in world history, which at its height stretched from Korea to Hungary, from Anatolia, Afghanistan and Burma to Siberia and north-west Russia (see map 1). Three out of the four khanates which rose after the dissolution of the empire in 1260 eventually embraced Islam. While toward the mid fourteenth century all of the khanates experienced political upheavals, which led to the dissolution of the khanates in China and Iran, the Muslim steppe khanates in Central Asia and southern Russia still had a long – and sometimes celebrated – history. This preserved the Chinggisids in the Muslim world up until the eve of the modern period.

One of the features that distinguishes the Mongols from the bearers of other steppe empires was that they continued to expand for several generations after the death of their founding father. The period of continued expansion was also the time in which Mongol imperial institutions, policies and ideology crystallized. Ögödei, Chinggis Khan's son and successor (r.1229–1241), played a leading role in both of these developments. Assuming the title Qa'an or Great Khan, Ögödei established his position as superior to his brothers who bore only the title khan, though he still stressed the collegial character of the empire. He founded the Mongol capital, Qara Qorum ("Black Sands") in the Orkhon valley in central Mongolia, the sacred territory of the Turks and Uighurs, and created the *jam* (Turkish: *yam*), the mounted postal courier system. Post stations were established at stages a day's journey apart (about every thirty-three to forty-five kilometers at a normal, somewhat leisurely, pace), and they provided horses, fodder and couriers for authorized travelers, who were able to cover about 350–400 km a day. The system enabled the Qa'an to transmit his orders efficiently and acquire information from the far reaches of the empire, in addition to securing the routes for ambassadors and merchants. Ögödei also shaped the central administration of the empire, employing professional administrators from the conquered regions, regulating revenue collection and

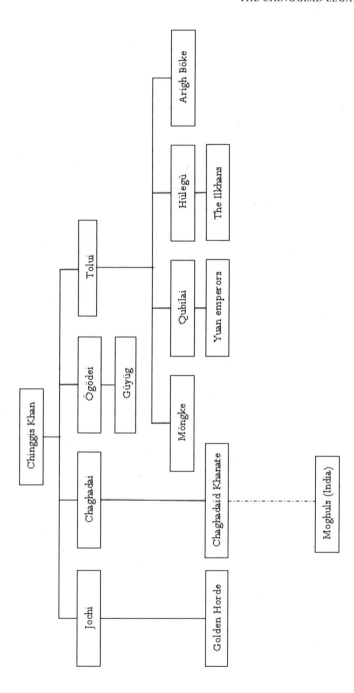

Figure 2. Main Descendants of Chinggis Khan

military recruitment, and differentiating between civil and military functions. The Mongol ideology of world conquest was further elaborated and openly proclaimed under Ögödei, contributing to a new wave of expansion. The Islamic world, however, did not rank high in Ögödei's plan of conquest, as his sights were set first on China and Europe.

In 1234 the Mongols annihilated Chinggis Khan's bitter enemy, the Jin dynasty, and in 1237–41 they wrought havoc in Europe, devastating southern Russia and Ukraine and reaching up to Germany before retreating back into Hungary. During all this time, a small Mongol force under the general Chormaqan operated in Iran, pursuing Jalal al-Din Khwarazm Shah, who was finally killed by locals in 1231 near Maragha in Azerbaijan. Thereafter, this same force continued to raid Iraq and al-Jazira (northern Mesopotamia) and subdued Georgia and Armenia. Following Ögödei's death, this contingent, now under the command of Baiju, advanced into Anatolia, defeating in 1243 the Seljuqs of Rum (who remained Mongol vassals till their extinction in 1307). This was achieved during the interregnum, which preceded the rise of Ögödei's eldest son Güyüg (r. 1246–1248) to the imperial throne, a period in which the Mongols were ruled by Ögödei's widow Töregena, and during which most expansion was halted. It was only in the 1250s, after the rise of a new Qa'an, Möngke, descendant of Ögödei's brother, Chinggis Khan's younger son, Tolui, that the Mongols advanced substantially into the Muslim world again.

Möngke rose to power after a bloody *coup d'état* in which the Toluids replaced the Ögödeids as the empire's rulers. His accession was followed by massive purges of the Ögödeid and Chaghadaid branches and their supporters, as well as by administrative reforms that furthered centralization. Through efficient use of censuses, Möngke was able to mobilize the resources of his vast realm and use it for further expansion. As leaders of the new campaigns he appointed his brothers: Qubilai was sent to China and Hülegü to the west, toward the Muslim world. Hülegü left Mongolia in 1253 and started his easy pace westwards, heading a multiethnic army whose composition, logistics and specialists reflected the height of Mongol ability to utilize people, knowledge, and goods for their aims. Hülegü's first destination was the home of the Assassins, a Shi'ite Isma'ili sect based in Alamut castle in the mountains of northern Iran and famed for their use of political murder for eliminating their rivals. When they threatened to assassinate the Qa'an, the Mongols assaulted. In 1256, after a series of long sieges, Hülegü defeated the Assassins, thereby achieving what many former Muslim rulers had tried in vain. His victory was celebrated by Muslim historians writing of the Mongols as a major contribution to Islam. Without meeting much opposition in Iran, Hülegü continued toward his next target, the Abbasid Caliph. In early 1258 Hülegü's forces stormed Baghdad and killed the last Caliph, who was supposedly wrapped in a carpet and trampled to death by the hooves of their horses. The bloody end to the Abbasid Caliphate, which had held sway for five hundred years and remained the main symbol of unity in the Muslim world, has been depicted ever since as the Mongols' greatest offence against Islam, although many Muslims, both Sunnis and Shiites, took part in Hülegü's conquest. Baghdad was also singled out for looting, arson, and destruction. This was due to the Caliph's haughty attitude toward the Mongols as well as his status as a universal ruler, and therefore competitor of the Mongol Qa'an. The fate of Baghdad was also due to the initiative of the many Christians (mainly Armenians and Georgians) who participated in the conquest of the Muslim sanctuary. By 1258, however, the devastation of Baghdad was the exception rather than the rule, for by Möngke's time Mongol campaigns were intentionally less destructive.

After Baghdad Hülegü turned to Syria, taking Aleppo and Damascus before his army was halted – for the first, but certainly not the last time – by the rising Mamluks (slave soldiers) of Egypt in the famous battle of ᶜAyn Jalut (modern Ein Harod in northern Israel) in 1260. It was perhaps not quite so impressive a feat as it may seem, for Hülegü had left with most of his troops before the battle to go to Azerbayjan and only a small part of his forces had remained to fight in Syria. Still, the battle justly earned a reputation as a turning point in the Mongol advance into the Muslim world, for logistical, political and military circumstances were such that the Mongols never managed to get beyond northern Iraq, except for a few months in 1300 in which they ruled Syria and Palestine.

Hülegü's departure for Azerbayjan was due to Möngke's demise in 1259 and its possible political implication on Hülegü's position. After Möngke's death, a fierce succession struggle ensued between his two

other brothers, Qubilai and Arigh Böqe. Their struggle greatly intensi-
fied the dissolution of the Mongol empire. The very size of the empire,
significantly increased under Hülegü and Qubilai, encouraged these divisions, as did the Chinggisid princes' growing identification with their
newly conquered regions. In contrast to the situation during the time of
Chinggis Khan, these were now mostly sedentary territories which did
not share the nomadic steppe tradition. Moreover, the Mongol expansion on all fronts had now come close to the ecological borders of the
steppe, a fact which made later expansion much more difficult.

At the end of the struggle, Möngke's successor, his brother Qubilai,
reaffirmed his position as Great Khan in 1264, and the empire was, for
all practical purposes, divided into four independent khanates. The
Khanate of the Great Khan, later known as Yuan dynasty (1271–1368),
was headed by Qubilai (r. 1260–1294) who moved the imperial capital
from Qara Qorum to Khanbaliq or Dadu, modern Beijing. He ruled
over northern and southern China (conquered in 1276–9), Manchuria,
Mongolia, parts of eastern Turkestan, and Tibet. Hülegü and his heirs,
known as Ilkhans ("the submissive khans," i.e. those who obey the Great

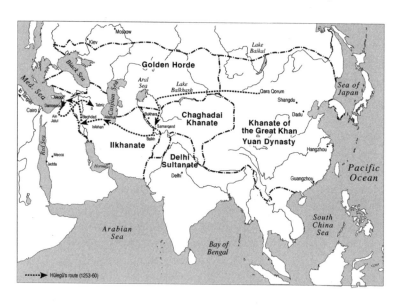

Map 4. The Four Mongol Khanates ca. 1290

Khan in China) ruled in the newly conquered regions in the Middle East
– Iran, Azerbaijan, Georgia, Armenia, Anatolia, and Iraq – territories
which Qubilai assigned to Hülegü in return for the latter's support of
Qubilai's cause against their brother Arigh Böqe. The Chaghadaid
Khanate, descendants of Chinggis Khan's second son, held power in
Central Asia, from Uighuria to the Oxus, i.e. from eastern Xinjiang to
the western border of Uzbekistan. The Golden Horde, the khanate
headed by the descendants of Chinggis Khan's eldest son Jochi, governed the Russian principalities, Eastern Europe to Hungary,
Khwarazm, the Qipchaq steppe, and Siberia eastward to the Irtish river
(see map 4). The division of the four khanates did not match the division
of Chinggis's land before his death. The Ögödeids, descendants of
Chinggis's successor, were deprived of any khanate, and despite the
heroic attempt of Ögödei's grandson, Qaidu (r. 1271–1301), to
reestablish an Ögödeid state in Central Asia, this political unit was swal-
lowed up by the Chaghadaid realm after his death. The Toluids held two
khanates: that of the Great Khan and the Ilkhanate established by Hülegü
and confirmed by Qubilai – not by Chinggis. These anomalies often
caused tensions and confrontations among the four khanates, but
despite the many – and often bloody – disputes among them, the
khanates were well aware of their common kinship and history.

Mongol dominion over Muslim lands began as infidel rule, but less
than a hundred years after Temüjin had been proclaimed Chinggis Khan,
his descendants began to embrace Islam. In 1295, with the rise of the
Ilkhan Ghazan (1295–1304), Islam became the state religion in Mongol
Iran, and the Ilkhans began to compete for the leadership of the Muslim
world. Around 1313, under the Golden Horde Khan Özbeg, Islam
became the state religion of the Golden Horde, thereby broadening the
abode of Islam and creating a strict boundary between the Muslim elite
of Turks and Mongols and their mostly Christian subjects. The
Chaghadaids in Transoxania embraced Islam in the 1330s, and it took a
few more decades for the Muslim religion to find its way into the eastern part of the Chaghadaid Khanate, known as Moghulistan. In China
and Mongolia, however, the Mongols adopted Tibetan Buddhism.

The golden age of the khanates was the latter half of the thirteenth
century and the beginning of the fourteenth. Toward the mid fourteenth

century, and certainly by the second half, they all began to encounter political problems. This led to the end of two of the four khanates and to important changes in the surviving two. The Ilkhanids were the first to fall, in 1335, though Mongol dynasties continued to rule in parts of the Ilkhanid realm into the late fourteenth century. In the 1380s, most of the original Ilkhanid realm became part of a new Turco-Mongolian empire, that of Tamerlane (see below). The Yuan dynasty in China followed the Ilkhanate in 1368, when it was overthrown by Chinese rebels who eventually established the Ming dynasty (1368–1644). Many Mongols, however, fled to Mongolia, where they retained their independence.

Around the mid-fourteenth century the Chaghadaid Khanate was divided into two parts: the western, Transoxania, and the eastern, known as Moghulistan ("land of the Mongols", encompassing modern north Kirgizstan, south Kazakhstan, and Xinjiang). Both parts witnessed a rise in the power of the emirs, military commanders, at the expense of the khans, a phenomenon which contributed to the fall of both the Ilkhanate and the Yuan. In the east, the khans of Moghulistan managed to reestablish their authority and control the emirs by the end of the fourteenth century, and they held power until the mid to late seventeenth century, when they were gradually replaced by Sufi sheikhs. Soon afterwards the region was absorbed into the emerging Qing dynasty (1644–1911) from China.

In the western part of the Chaghadaid Khanate, the actual power remained with the emirs, mainly due to the rise of Tamerlane (r. 1370–1405), a Turco-Mongol Muslim emir who soon emerged as the de facto leader of Transoxania, and aspired to revive the Mongol empire. Not being a descendant of Chinggis Khan, Tamerlane (Persian: Timur-i lang, Temür the Lame) could not assume the title khan. He was known as emir, military commander, and, after marrying several Chinggisid princesses, also as *küregen* (Mongolian: son-in-law). Through most of his rule he set up Chinggisid khans as puppet rulers and also assembled a host of Mongol princes of the different branches in his court, portraying himself as their patron.

While he also used Islam as a major element of legitimation, Tamerlane consciously tried to imitate Chinggis Khan: he plundered both Russia and India and died on his way to conquer China. Part of his imitation was the practice of deliberate destruction, and the towers of skulls he left behind him won a worldwide fame, surpassing even Chinggis's reputation for devastation. Moreover, like Chinggis, Tamerlane succeeded in consolidating his personal charisma. In Central Asia he became a source of prestige, myth and legitimation second only to Chinggis Khan himself (see chapter five). Tamerlane's political and institutional achievements, however, were much less impressive than Chinggis's, and his empire began to shrink and disintegrate soon after his death. Tamerlane's descendants ruled in Transoxania and Khurasan throughout the fifteenth century. Their political weakness compensated for by the artistic and architectural flowering in their realm, their reign was known as the Timurid renaissance. This period also witnessed the rise of the Eastern Turkic literary language called Chaghatay, after the turkicized form of the name of Chinggis Khan's second son, Chaghaday, as a major literary language. This is the only case in which a Mongolian name became attached to an element of high culture. Many of the modern Central Asian tongues (Uzbek, Kazakh, Uighur) developed from the Chaghatay language.

The Timurids also established matrimonial relations with the Chinggisids in Moghulistan. They were finally driven out of Transoxania in the early sixteenth century by the Uzbeks, a Chinggisid-led people originating in the Golden Horde (about which see below). One Timurid prince, Babur, descendant of Tamerlane by his father and of Chinggis Khan by his Moghul mother, escaped to Afghanistan. In 1526 he conquered Delhi and founded the Moghul (or Mughal) dynasty which ruled in India until 1858. This name for Babur and his heirs derives from the fact that in post-thirteenth-century India any invader from the south was called Moghul; the Turkic form of the word Mongol. They, however, called themselves al-Timuriya, the Timurids. (The legendary wealth of the Moghuls in the sixteenth to seventeenth centuries gave birth later to the English 'Mogul,' a rich and successful businessman.)

The mid fourteenth century saw also the rise of the emirs in the Golden Horde realm. Moreover, in 1380 those emirs suffered a major – and first – defeat by a coalition of Russian princes in the battle of Kulikovo, near Moscow. Soon afterwards the Khan Toqtamiish (r.1381–1395), a Chinggisid prince who had begun his career as

Tamerlane's protégé, managed to reestablish Chinggisid rule in the Golden Horde and overcome the Russian challenge. His success, however, threatened his non-Chinggisid patron. In 1395 Tamerlane invaded the Golden Horde, burned and looted its capital, Sarai, and advanced to the gates of Moscow. The Golden Horde survived for another century, but its disintegration soon became apparent as it found it more difficult to maintain its superiority vis-à-vis the emerging power of Muscovy and Lithuania on the one hand, and its internal cohesion on the other. Major splits in the Golden Horde occurred during the fifteenth century: in 1438 it was divided into the khanate of Kazan and "the Great Horde." A further division in 1441 brought about the creation of the Khanates of Astrakhan and Crimea in two of the most urban and sedentary parts of the Golden Horde. At the same time various splinter groups from the Golden Horde's steppe regions, mainly the Uzbeks, Kazakhs, and Nogais, began to coalesce and assert their independence. The Great Horde was destroyed by the Khanate of Crimea (itself under Ottoman overlordship from 1475) in 1502, but part of its territory had already been taken by the rising Moscow, the nucleus of Tsarist Russia. Kazan and Astrakhan fell to Ivan the Terrible in 1552 and 1554, and in 1783 Catherine the Great annexed the Khanate of Crimea. Most of the Golden Horde Muslim population, however, retained their separate identity under Russian rule.

Simultaneously with the fall of the Great Horde, in the early sixteenth century, the Uzbeks, the main nomadic splinter group of the Golden Horde, completed their migration southward, taking over Transoxania from the Timurids in 1501. The Uzbeks revived Chinggisid rule in the region, consciously holding up Chinggis as their model, and they held power in Central Asia until the 1920s, although their Chinggisid leadership collapsed in the mid to late eighteenth century. The Kazakhs, another Chinggisid branch that separated from the Uzbeks in the mid fifteenth century, took over some of the territory of Moghulistan, and perpetuated Chinggisid rule in Central Asia up to the nineteenth century.

In short, despite the decline of the Mongol khanates in the fourteenth century, Chinggisid dynasties continued to be part of the Muslim world until the modern era.

BROADENING MUSLIM HORIZONS: CROSS-CULTURAL CONTACTS AND THEIR SIGNIFICANCE

The Mongol successor states were only one facet of the Mongol legacy. Another, and perhaps the most significant, consequence was the globalizing effect of the Mongol empire and the cross-cultural exchange both inside and outside the empire that it inspired. Certainly the vast dimensions of the empire contributed to this, but the Mongols were not simply a passive medium through which the sophisticated sedentary subjects learnt from one another. Instead, through their imperial policies and active support of international trade, the Mongols actively promoted inter-cultural exchange which influenced the Muslim world as well as other parts of Eurasia.

The Mongols' active role originally derived from the fact that the formation of the empire, its continued expansion, and the establishment of its administration required a huge mobilization of people throughout the empire. This mobilization was the first step toward cross-cultural exchange and integration. The mobilization can be explained primarily by demographic considerations. During the time of Chinggis Khan, the total population of Mongolia numbered approximately 700,000. Therefore, human capital was of primary importance to the nomads, and the political struggles that accompanied the formation of the Mongol state concentrated on the control of people and herds rather than territorial gains. The demographic balance also meant that in order to continue to expand, the Mongols had to make use of the already conquered (and submitted) subjects. The first and perhaps most wide-ranging means for Mongol mobilization was therefore the army. Hence Chinggis Khan appropriated defeated nomads and tribes, organized in new decimal units, among Mongol princes and commanders and sent them to fight across Eurasia: a process that continued on an even larger scale in the campaigns of his heirs.

Mobilization was not limited to the military sphere. As soon as the Mongols found themselves rulers of an empire with a significant sedentary sector, they realized they lacked not only numbers but also specialists. They therefore looked for experts and collected and redistributed them across Eurasia, regarding human talent (from both inside and outside the empire) as a form of booty, to be shared among family members like material goods. This process involved groups – such as the 100,000 artisans taken in 1221 from Transoxiana to Mongolia and China, and the northern Chinese farmers sent to Merv and later transferred to Azerbaijan – as well as (many) individuals, specializing in various fields. These included military specialists like the two siege engineers Isma'il and Jalal al-Din who were sent by the Ilkhan Abaqa to Qubilai, and were instrumental in the Mongol conquest of southern China; leading religious figures, such as the Daoist monk Chang Chun, summoned by Mongol khans; physicians, astronomers, interpreters, technicians, cooks and even athletes. Möngke once sent Hülegü his best Mongolian wrestler requesting him to find a worthy local rival, thereby instituting one of the very first international championship sporting matches.

The collection of specialists was systematized already in the late 1230s by means of census, which classified people according to their skills (such as military and artisan). Later on, the different khanates competed for these specialists and exchanged them in order to better control and exploit the economic and cultural resources of their sedentary possessions and to enhance their kingly reputation.

The mobilization process was often painful – the Samarqandi artisans transferred to northern China probably mourned their fate, the ruin of their homeland and the murder of their kin, rather then rejoiced at the opportunity to exchange artistic techniques with their Chinese colleagues – but at the same time that the Mongols were mercilessly destroying human and cultural resources, they were also creating conditions in which long-distance cultural exchange flourished.

The Mongol policy of ruling through foreign specialists also encouraged mobilization and exchange. Originating in Mongol numerical inferiority and their fear of potential local resistance, this policy was already practiced by Chinggis Khan (see chapter three). It was further systematized and documented in Yuan China, where the Mongols created a special category of *semuren* (people of various kinds), second only to the Mongols and more privileged than their Chinese subjects, for their foreign (non-Chinese and non-Mongol) subjects. Yet many foreigners were also active in the other Mongol khanates. The Mongols preferred foreigners who originated in the inter-regional nomadic empires, i.e. who were not only skilled in the laws of the cities but also had connections to the steppe (e.g. Khitans, Uighurs, Khwarazmians), though other talented people were also welcome (the most famous example being Marco Polo). In order to secure the loyalty of these foreigners, the Mongols aspired to give them "a taste of home," and therefore brought foreign (mostly Muslim or Central Asian) food, medicine and entertainment into Yuan China. While the situation in China is far better documented than that in the other khanates, a certain presence of Far Eastern food, medicine, knowledge and entertainment was attested to in Mongol Iran and apparently also in the Chaghadaid Khanate and in the Golden Horde.

Most of what was transmitted throughout the empire was not the Mongols' own culture but rather elements of the culture of their sedentary subjects. However, it was the Mongols who initiated the bulk of these exchanges. Most of these bearers of culture were agents of the empire (e.g. diplomats, merchants, administrators, artisans, soldiers or hostages). The Mongols also served as a filter, determining which particular cultural goods would be diffused across Eurasia. They showed great interest in fields that were compatible with their own norms, notably with their shamanistic beliefs, such as astronomy, divination, medicine (i.e. healing) and geomancy, and thus also promoted scientific transfers. In short, the flow of people, ideas and goods across Asia was determined to a large extent by what the Mongols liked, needed and were interested in. Persian astronomers, for instance, arrived in Yuan China not because they or their Chinese counterparts sought scientific exchange, but because the Mongols wanted a second opinion on the reading of Heaven's portents (Allsen 2001: 211).

Trade was, obviously, another means of promoting cross-cultural exchange, and the Mongols played an active role here too by promoting long-distance commerce. The process of state formation among the nomads in itself stimulated trade through an increased demand for precious metals, gems, and especially fine cloth. All of these were needed to assert authority in a newly formed polity. Chinggis Khan was certainly aware of the benefit of commerce (which indirectly led to the

Khwarazm campaign), and Muslim merchants were among his earliest supporters, joining his side even before he completed the unification of Mongolia. Moreover, after the early conquests, the Mongol elite, the main beneficiaries of the booty brought in by the conquests, became extremely wealthy. They recycled this wealth by investing in their commercial agents, the *ortogh*, who were mostly Muslims and Uighurs. The *ortogh* was a trader (or trading company) who acted on behalf of, or who was financed by the capital of, a Mongol (or other) notable in return for a share of the profit. The profits were used for the lavish consumption characteristic of the "nouveaux riches." The establishment of Qara Qorum also promoted trade since the resources of the Mongolian homeland could hardly support a big city (by the standards of the steppe). The Mongols were ready to pay generously for the privilege of remaining in the steppe while at the same time enjoying the best of the agricultural world. Many traders eagerly exploited these opportunities, benefiting from the safe roads and the access to the post stations. Even after the dissolution of the empire into the four khanates, Mongol governments continued to promote both local and international trade, which provided taxes, markets, profits, and prestige. The khanates competed for commercial specialists, provided infrastructure for transcontinental travel, and were even actively involved in the manipulation of bullion flow. Mongol capitals in Azerbaijan, the Volga region, Central Asia and northern China became hubs of international markets. Other cities, first in Mongolia and later mainly in northern China, became centers of artisanship and industry for the expanding empire. New cities, centers of commercial exchange, materialized along the Silk Roads, especially in the Volga region but also in Central Asia.

At the same time as land routes flourished during the *Pax Mongolica*, the maritime routes also thrived. The Indian Ocean, for example, was a central route for trade between China, India and Iran; and the Black Sea and Mediterranean connected the Golden Horde with Mamluk Egypt, Byzantium and Western Europe, and the Ilkhanate with the Italian city states. Muslims from inside and outside the empire continued to play a leading role among the merchants, but Uighurs, Chinese and Europeans were also amongst those who benefited from the open world of the Chinggisids. While long-distance trade was usually conducted in relays before the Mongol period (that is, traders only traveled from station A to B and transferred their goods there to another merchant who continued to station C, and so on), under Mongol rule people often traveled the entire length of the Silk Routes – the notable example again being Marco Polo. The trade routes encompassed regions vaster than the empire: India maintained close commercial ties with Iran, China and Central Asia (especially after the Islamization of Transoxania) and the Italian city states held colonies in the Ilkhanate and the Golden Horde and took an active part in the trade to Central and East Asia.

What effect did these cross cultural contacts have on life in the Muslim world? The wide-range mobilization and the expanding trade led to the frequent and continuous movement of people, goods, ideas, technologies, knowledge, plants, and even germs, throughout Eurasia, thereby encouraging Eurasian integration. The best evidence of the growth of knowledge about the world in the Muslim realm under Mongol rule comes from Iran. The Ilkhanate had especially close relations with Yuan China. They were ruled by the same Chinggisid branch and were closely connected politically and economically. Moreover, both were heirs to ancient civilizations, and they shared their cultural resources in fields as various as historiography, medicine, military technology, geography, cartography, astronomy, and painting. One of the best examples of the broadening of Muslim horizons under the Mongols was Rashid al-Din's *Jami' al-tawarikh* ("Collection of Chronicles"), the first true world history to be written in the Muslim world or, for that matter, anywhere else. Rashid al-Din (d. 1318), a physician of Jewish origin, who probably began to serve the Mongols in the early 1290s, served as the co-vizier under the Ilkhans Ghazan (r. 1295–1304) and Öljeitü (r. 1304–1316), and was one of the main cultural brokers active in the Ilkhanid court. Ghazan ordered him to write a history of the Mongols, and later, at Öljeitü's insistence, this was extended to the history of all the nations in the known world. Indeed, *The Collection of Chronicles* included more than a detailed history of the Mongols from the pre-Chinggisid period to the rise of Chinggis Khan and the reigns of his successors up to Temür Öljeitü, Qubilai's successor (partially based on Mongol sources accessible to Rashid al-Din through his friend Bolad, a

Mongol who had served as Qubilai's emissary in Iran). The collection also included sections dedicated to the history of China, India, the Muslim world, the Jews, and the Franks, as well as detailed genealogical and geographical appendices. The book was compiled with the help of oral informants and written sources derived from the nations in question. It was put together by a committee of research assistants working under Rashid al-Din, in a way quite similar to the manner in which official histories were compiled in China. The result was a quantum leap in the knowledge of the world available in the Muslim Middle East, especially concerning China, Mongolia and East Asia at large. The book was highly popular, and while there was hardly any continuation to Rashid al-Din's histories of the nations, the history of the Mongols, including that of Chinggis Khan and his infidel (and Muslim) heirs, became an integral part of general histories of the Muslim world (see chapter five).

Another field in which cross-cultural contacts had a lasting effect in the Muslim world was the field of art, especially painting. Mongol rule led to a combination of two pre-Mongol Muslim traditions: the Byzantine-influenced style developed in Baghdad and the Seljuq or Turco-Iranian prevalent in Iran, both enriched by the fruits of the encounter with East Asian art. Chinese influence on Persian painting in the Mongol period is obvious, especially in landscape painting, which reflected new concepts of space developed by Yuan painters, but also in motifs, symbols and themes. The Ilkhanid period (just like the Yuan period in China) was a time of great development and activity in painting, especially in the field of illuminated manuscripts, characterized by larger pictures (partly due to the improved paper arriving from China) and more paintings in a manuscript. The new forms and methods created in Iran were disseminated throughout the Islamic world and continued into the Timurid period, to become the standard of quality painting from the Ottoman empire to Central Asia and Moghul India.

Not all the imported knowledge was warmly received. After all, it was connected to the alien rulers and often came too soon and too fast. A notable example was the failure of the Ilkhans to institute the use of paper money in Iran. A well-established means of exchange in China, paper money was adopted in Iran in the 1290s under the guidance of Qubilai's representative, Bolad, and was intended to solve the monetary problems of the Ilkhanid court: the court claimed a monopoly on precious metals and tried to force its subjects to exchange their coins with the new paper currency. Despite the draconian measures taken to enforce the new monetary system, it was a complete failure. People refused to give up coins and the attempt to enforce the use of the paper money led to a halt in trade, which forced the Ilkhan Geikhatu to end the experiment after a mere two months. Paper money was not reintroduced in the Muslim Middle East until the modern period. However, the repercussions of this experiment went beyond currency, for it was in connection with paper money that printing was first introduced into the Middle East. By rejecting the paper money, the Muslims surrendered the use of printing, and this was one of the reasons why printing remained absent from the Muslim Middle East until the late eighteenth century, when it was adopted under European influence. Certainly, not all, or even most, of what was displayed in Iran due to the broad horizons of the Mongols was adopted, but the assimilation of certain crops, food and customs is apparent.

The period also saw the expansion of Muslim arts (especially textile and performing arts), cuisine, science (such as medicine, astronomy, mathematics) and military technology into China. We have much less information about the situation in the Chaghadaid Khanate or the Golden Horde, but there is enough evidence to attest to the broadening of connections and exchange in their realms too, and the resulting cultural influence.

Moreover, the Mongol "globalization" also had an impact on Muslim life beyond the frontiers of the Mongol Empire. Apart from the general expansion of Islam discussed below, two prime examples are the travels of Ibn Battuta and the Yemeni dictionary known as the *Hexaglot* (i.e. "six languages"). Ibn Battuta (1304–1368/9) was born in Tangier, Morocco, far from Mongol rule. In 1324 he left his hometown to perform the pilgrimage to Mecca, in what turned out to be the beginning of some 30 years of travel which led him around most of the then-known world, including, according to his claims, the entire Middle East, the Qipchaq steppe, Afghanistan, Central Asia, India, China, South-East Asia, Africa and southern Europe, a greater distance than Marco Polo or any other traveler of the period covered. During his travels, he visited all of the four Mongol khanates. Such an unprecedented and lengthy journey was made possible mainly due to the "global" world created by the Chinggisids. The travelogue that Ibn Battuta prepared after his return home acquired immediate popularity. It included brief accounts of the places he had visited and his adventures there, supplemented by notes which reflected his major fields of interest: saintly men and their tombs, rulers, women and food. The information Ibn Battuta provided is not always reliable – he often depended on previous sources without acknowledging them, and at times confused historical and chronological details – yet some of his descriptions (of East Africa, southern India, the Maldives, Mali, the Chaghadaid Khanate) are particularly invaluable because there are few other sources for these areas from this time. He is also a major source for understanding the Islamic scene in the Mongol khanates in the early fourteenth century. More important for our purposes here, Ibn Battuta's *Rihla* ("Journey") greatly broadened North African (and other Muslim regions') knowledge of the world. Indeed, in North Africa, his descriptions remained the basis for information on the Mongols, China, and India for centuries.

Another example of the broadening of Muslim horizons in the Mongol period is the *King's Dictionary*, prepared in Yemen of the 1360s by one of the rulers of the Rasulid dynasty (1228–1454). The Sunni Rasulids were one of a number of Turkic dynasties that came to power during the decline of the Seljuqs. Named after Muhammad b. Harun who had served as a messenger (*rasul*) in the service of the Abbasids, they arrived in Yemen with their overlords, the Ayyubids, in the late twelfth century and emerged as an independent kingdom after the Ayyubids' departure of the region in the 1220s. The dynasty made full use of the opportunities opened by Mongol rule, and Marco Polo and Ibn Battuta both attest to the thriving commerce in Aden, the Rasulid capital, in the thirteenth to fourteenth centuries. The dictionary was compiled by the king al-Malik al-Afdal 'Abbas b. 'Ali (r. 1363–1377), famous as a man of learning rather than as a warrior or statesman. It includes vocabularies in no less than six languages: Arabic, Persian, Turkic, Mongol, Greek and Armenian, the major political, commercial and cultural languages of the eastern Mediterranean and western Asia during the Mongol era. Beginning with the name of God (Allah, translated as *Tengri* in Mongolian and Turkic), the dictionary consists of lists of vocabulary in various fields (such as heaven and earth, human body, kinship terms, time and seasons, geography, textile, plants, food and drink, animals; colors, weapon, and numbers. The *Hexaglot* was composed after Ilkhanid rule in Iran had already come to its end, yet it was done under cultural influences stemming from the Chinggisid world, being part of a tradition of multi-lingual dictionaries encouraged by the Mongols. The Mongols used several languages and scripts in the management of their empire, and this feature acted as a major catalyst in the growth of language study throughout Eurasia. They generously rewarded those with linguistic skills, and mastery of both Mongolian (in its spoken or written forms) and foreign languages often conferred status and power. The Mongols organized schools for language training, encouraged translation and sponsored or inspired the compilation of multi-lingual vocabularies. Although the *Hexaglot* is unique in the number and combination of languages registered, it is quite representative of its age, for we find multi-lingual lists of terms appearing in Iran, China, Armenia, Korea, North India, Egypt, and Crimea. The major beneficiary of this linguistic cosmopolitanism was Persian, which was studied simultaneously in China, Crimea and Italy in the thirteenth to fourteenth centuries. This was a most appropriate choice since it was already the language of learning in a wide area stretching from Central Asia to Anatolia.

The existence of travel literature and dictionaries was not just the result of cross-cultural contacts, it also facilitated further contacts. In the thirteenth and fourteenth centuries this led to a growing degree of Eurasian integration. The closer ties were loosened somewhat after the fall of the Mongol khanates in Iran and (especially) in China, not the least due to the effects of the Black Death, the fast spread of which was also due to this integration. But in at least some fields (e.g., art, historiography, cuisine) the integration of Eurasia had a lasting effect on post-Mongol Muslim culture.

The Expansion of Islam

Juwayni (d. 1283), writing before the Islamization of any of the Mongol states, mentions that there had been a notable expansion of the realm of Islam in the wake of the Mongol conquests. He attributes this to the flourishing trade and contacts encouraged by the Mongols as well as to their tolerant attitude toward religions in general (Juwayni, 1997: 13–19). The first expansion of Islam at the time was eastward. Though it never became the dominant religion in either Mongolia or China, three of the four Mongol khanates embraced Islam, thereby accelerating its diffusion in eastern Central Asia, China, and the East European steppes. Indirectly the Mongols also contributed to the Islamization of more distant regions such as India, South-East Asia, and even Africa, mainly by accelerating Muslim presence there.

The Islamization of the three Mongol khanates (the Ilkhanate in the late thirteenth century, and the Golden Horde and the Chaghadaid Khanate in the early to mid fourteenth century) was a long and complex process, stemming mainly from the close and continuous contact between the Mongols and their Muslim subjects, most notably the Turkish officers and soldiers, who were the bulk of the Mongol armies. Conversion stories give the impression that Mongol islamization began with a royal conversion and then spread from the top down. However, at least in the cases of the Ilkhanate and the Chaghadaids, the process seems to have started at the bottom, among the rank and file of the army – mainly due to acculturation, intermarriage and the activity of charismatic preachers – and then moved upward. While the role of spirituality or inner conviction in conversion dynamics cannot be denied, obviously political motives also played a part, at least in the rulers' conversion. In the Ilkhanate, for instance, the conversion of the Ilkhan Ghazan (1295–1304) took place during his struggle to win the crown and secured him the alliance of a leading commander – a Muslim Mongol – as well as Muslim segments of the army. Moreover, the annihilation of the Caliphate meant that there was no proclaimed leader for the Muslim world (as the Pope was for much of the Christian world). Thus, when the Mongols embraced Islam, they could easily join the competition for Muslim leadership. Furthermore, as Muslims, the Mongols enjoyed a legitimacy that no infidel rulers could hope for in the eyes of their Muslim subjects, and this might have been another incentive for their conversion, at least in the Ilkhanate (or, at any rate, a favorable by-product). In the Golden Horde, by contrast, the Mongols' adoption of Islam emphasized the distinction between them and their Christian

Russian subjects, drawing them instead closer to the Turks of the region. Another factor which facilitated conversion was Sufi activity. The Sufis, with their stress on tolerance toward other religious traditions and their skill in "magic" (perhaps not dissimilar to the shaman's role) were portrayed as the agents behind the royal conversions, and they have retained their central position as agents of Islamization ever since. Royal conversions, and the campaigns against infidels which usually followed them (such as the intermittent persecution of Buddhism in Iran during Ghazan's reign), further consolidated the position of Islam in the Mongol khanates. While in the Ilkhanate most of the population was already Muslim, the conversion of the Chaghadaid Khans and of the Golden Horde caused Islam to be carried further into the steppes of Central Asia, and Eastern Europe. The mid-fourteenth-century Islamization of the Mongols thus resulted in the emergence of a new Turco-Mongolian elite in the region that lies between the Tian Shan mountains (in East Central Asia, in Kyrgyzstan and China) and the Volga. This elite was Muslim, spoke Turkish and honored the traditions of the Mongol empire. It is difficult to recall another era in which so vast a territory has shared so much in terms of language, religion and culture.

As mentioned above, the Mongol state in China never embraced Islam, but the Mongol period none the less led to a considerable increase in the Muslim presence in China and contributed to its proliferation all over the country, establishing long-lasting Muslim communities in north, northwest, and southwest China. The Muslims arrived in China through two main ways: as conscripts or as free agents. The conscripts were mainly the thousands of artisans whom the Mongols deported to the east from Chinggis's time onward. Many of them were Central Asians, primarily from Transoxania, who had formerly been sent to Qara Qorum but were moved to northern China when Qubilai transferred the Mongol capital from Qara Qorum to Shangdu and later to Khanbaliq (Beijing). Among those who arrived voluntarily, traders formed an important group. Originally attracted by the commercial opportunities in the Mongol empire, many of them, including those who came from Iraq and Syria, chose to settle in China on a permanent basis, thereby establishing new communities along the trade routes. The regular contact between China and the Muslim world during the period first of the United Empire and thereafter of the Yuan dynasty and the Ilkhanate assured a constant flow of Muslim experts into China, some of them remaining there. Mongol policies of ruling through strangers also meant that many Muslims could find lucrative offices in Yuan administration, where they came to play a leading role, especially in the financial administration under Qubilai. Most famous among them was Ahmad (d. 1282), a Central Asian who became Qubilai's major financial adviser and his left prime minister (the second highest post in Yuan administration), before being assassinated by his envious Chinese opponents. Another arena in which Muslims were especially active was the Yuan local administration. Here the most prominent example is Sayyid Ajall (1210–1279), a descendant of a notable Bukharan family who had already served the Mongols during Ögödei's reign. In 1271 Sayyid Ajall was appointed as Qubilai's governor in Yunnan, in southwest China, a tribal frontier area which had hitherto formed an independent kingdom known as Dali. Sayyid Ajall and his descendants, who succeeded him, managed to draw this area into the Chinese cultural sphere, where it has remained ever since, mainly by promoting Confucian learning. At the same time, however, they also promoted Islam. Sayyid Ajall attracted many Muslims to the southwest and converted some of its original population. The significant contemporary Chinese-Muslim community in Yunnan traces its origin to him, and Zheng He, the famous Muslim admiral who led the Chinese navy in its unprecedented voyages in the fifteenth century, is also considered to be his descendant.

Conversion was another means through which Muslim presence in China increased. Rashid al-Din recounts that Qubilai's grandson, who bore the Buddhist name Ananda and who governed the former Tangut country, embraced Islam and managed to convert most of the 150,000 Mongol troops under his command. The Gansu-Ninxia region in northwest China where Ananda was stationed has remained a center of Chinese Islam to this day. In general, one can note that before the Yuan dynasty, Muslims in China were mainly concentrated in the ports on the south-east coast, having arrived by the maritime trade routes, whereas from the Yuan period onward there were important Muslim communities inland as well, especially in the north, northwest and southwest, where many of them have endured until the present.

Less directly, the Mongol period also led to the further expansion of Islam into India. Chinggis Khan's invasion of Central Asia caused many Central Asian Muslims to flee southward, into the subcontinent. Many of the refugees were well-educated. The most famous among them is the historian Juzjani, who later wrote a detailed description of the Mongols from his refuge in Delhi, unsurprisingly depicting them in a hostile vein. Juzjani and the many other scholars who followed the same route contributed significantly to the Muslim culture of the newly-established Delhi Sultanate.

Later immigrants from the Chaghadaid and Ilkhanid realms also increased the Muslim presence in India. When worsted in some conflict with their confreres, Mongols and their subjects often sought asylum in Delhi, and already in the late thirteenth century an entire quarter of the capital was called *Chinggisi* after them. If not already Muslims, they converted after their arrival, to be known as Neo-Muslims. Often military leaders, they became a significant element in the political life of the sultanate. Waves of immigrants continued to arrive in Delhi in the fourteenth century, often in conjunction with the fate of Islam in the Chaghadaid realm: Ibn Battuta reports that after the deposition of Tarmashirin (Chaghadaid Muslim khan 1331–1334), 40,000 (i.e. a large number) of his Muslim supporters, including commanders of *tümens* and hundreds, migrated to Delhi. Another group of Khurasani emirs arrived in 1342–3, perhaps after the deposition of the Muslim Halil Sultan. These Mongol soldiers contributed to the expansion of the Delhi Sultanate into south India. The expansion of the maritime trade caused by the commercial policies of the Mongols also led to the establishment of large Muslim communities in south Indian ports, mainly Gujarat. Some of these communities later played an important role in the conversion of additional regions.

More indirectly still, the Mongols contributed to the spread of Islam into other regions, mainly South East Asia and Africa. It began to thrive there, at least in the East African case, long before the Mongol period (as was the case in China and India), but since the main agents of Islamization were traders, the flourishing commerce in the Mongol empire gave the process a considerable boost. Thus Marco Polo observed that the kingdom of Perlak in northern Sumatra "is so much frequented by the Saracen (i.e. Muslim) merchants that they have converted the natives to the law of Muhammad," and by the end of the thirteenth century we have further evidence of the beginning of Islamization in Malay and Java. Some of the agents of conversion were Muslims from China and India (Gujarat), often people who came eastward or southward due to Mongol upheavals. In a similar manner, the growing Muslim commercial activity resulted in the further spreading of Islam into Africa, mainly in Mali, Zanzibar and Zimbabwe, to name but a few places.

The Islamization of these regions was far from complete in the thirteenth century. Marco Polo mentions that only the town people converted in Perlak: the hill dwellers were still living like beasts. Accordingly, Ibn Battuta was rather frustrated in his attempts to enforce Muslim law (especially women's modest attire) in the Maldive islands or in Mali in Africa. Gradually, however, the traders, often complemented by Sufis, on the one hand, and economic and political benefits that the elite derived from being part of a universal Muslim community on the other, led to the further consolidation of Islam in these regions, often with lasting results. Perhaps the best proof for the expansion and vitality of the Muslim world in the Mongol period is that Ibn Battuta was able to travel so widely throughout Asia and Africa and still feel at home wherever he went (except for China and Sardinia); he could even make a living as a Muslim judge during most of his travels.

Geopolitical and Ethnic Changes

Despite the tendency of Muslim and Russian thinkers (as well as some Chinese nationalists in the early twentieth century) to ascribe everything that went wrong with their civilizations to the Mongols' influence, the Mongols did not make drastic changes in the Eurasian geopolitical balance. The initial invasions were traumatic enough, but the destruction was limited in both its extent and duration. As soon as the Mongols understood that they could get more from their lands by taxing them instead of ravaging them – and this was apparent already during the reign of Chinggis's grandson, Möngke (1251–1259) – they consciously attempted to limit the damage. This does not mean that there were no exceptions, and the bloody conquest of Baghdad in 1258 is by far the most famous example. Furthermore, regions that became buffer areas between the Mongols and their enemies (such as Iraq, especially al-Jazira) or later between the rival Mongol khanates (Khurasan and Uighuria) certainly suffered from multiple raids throughout the thirteenth to early fourteenth centuries, and regions which the nomads turned into full pasture lands (e.g., Moghulistan) were badly harmed even in the long run. Yet together with the calculated or accidental devastation, there were also positive attempts by the Mongol khans to restore the productivity of their lands, attempts that were facilitated by the multiple possibilities of regional and international trade. World historians therefore agree that in general the Muslim Middle East and China retained their status as the world's leading productive regions, both during and after the Mongol conquests (Abu Lukhod 1989, 352 ff; Frank 1998, 75–84, 108–116).

Mongol rule was, however, geopolitically important in two ways. First, it led to a shifting of the political center in most regions included in the empire, sometimes with lasting results. Second, the administrative divisions that turned into four separate Mongol khanates after 1260 were influential in shaping later political boundaries and ethnic identities. Both were certainly felt in the Muslim world.

Mongol rule led to a changing of the capital of each of the established khanates, mostly in the general direction of north-east. This might have originally reflected the location of Qara Qorum, the Mongol capital on the Orkhon river, or the nomads' need to reside closer to the steppe. For example, this meant that the capital of the eastern Islamic world shifted from Baghdad to Tabriz in Iran's Azerbaijan (see map 3). Tabriz remained Iran's capital till the late sixteenth century, and the Timurids, the Qara and Aq Qoyunlu, and the Safawids competed for control over it, due more to its prestige than to its strategic or economic value. Even after the Safawids established their capital in Isfahan, Tabriz remained a privileged city, being, for instance, the residence of the Iranian heir apparent until the early twentieth century. The ephemeral capitals of Mongol Central Asia did not have an enduring legacy, but in the other Mongol khanates this process had more lasting effects, leading to the rise of Beijing in China and to the importance of Moscow – not a seat of a Mongol court but the leader of the Mongols' subject principalities – in Russia.

Mongol rule in Iran also contributed to the emergence of that country as a distinct political and ethnic entity within the Muslim world. The use of the name Iran to denominate a political entity, a Sasanian concept not used during early Muslim rule in Iran, was revived under the Mongols. This fulfilled their wish to find an adequate denomination of their ulus which would not stress their abnormal position vis-à-vis the other Mongol khanates. Under Ilkhanid rule, the Persian language gained supremacy over Arabic as a vehicle for writing history in the eastern Muslim world and soon became the written *lingua franca* of the Turco-Mongolic world. The pre-Islamic Persian past, as recounted in the *Book of Kings*, enjoyed a renewed interest and, in its illuminated versions prepared for the Ilkhans, the Persian kings and heroes were dressed in Mongol attire, thereby stressing Mongol identification with Iran's pre-Islamic past. The orientation of the Ilkhanate toward China revived the close connections between Iran and the East, more apparent in the Sasanid period than in the Abbasid one. Even the Ilkhanate's borders were closer to those of the Sasanid empire (and of modern Iran). In ethnic terms, the Mongol conquests brought a wave of Central Asian nomads into Iran. These mostly Turkic elements remained in the region after the dissolution of the Ilkhanate and have become a consistent element of Iran's multi-ethnic population and society. Moreover, until the end of the nineteenth century these Turkic nomads and post-nomads, which eventually included many of the Mongols who remained in Iran, held much of the political and military power in Iran (Fragner 1997).

As for the rest of the Middle East, the Mongol annihilation of the Abbasid Caliphate in Baghdad, turned Iraq – once the center of the Islamic world – into the provincial backwater it remained in later centuries. Under the Mamluks, whose state was the only Muslim entity that successfully defied the Mongols, Egypt increased its position as an alternative, leading center of the Muslim world, and the establishment and consolidation of the Mamluk regime owed much to its successful struggle against the Ilkhanate. Even the *beylik* (principality) of Uthman (known in Turkish as Osman), later to become the Ottoman Empire, rose inside the Ilkhanid sphere of influence. A recent controversial article goes so far as to suggest that the Ottomans originated from Golden Horde refugees (Heywood 2000). In general, the Mongol period completed the process of Turco-Mongol (as opposed to Arab or Persian) dominance of the ruling elites of the Middle East, a process which had begun as early as the ninth century.

The legacy of the other Muslim khanates, the Chaghadaid state and the Golden Horde, is more complex. The Golden Horde is often described as the nucleus of Muscovy and Russia as a Eurasian empire, which, however, rose not from the Golden Horde but out of its debris. The Chaghadaid Khanate has no modern counterpart, although, as mentioned above, it did give birth to the empire of Tamerlane and indirectly to the Moghul dynasty in India. Yet in terms of ethnic changes, the impact of the Mongol period was most apparent in Central Asia, and many of the Muslim people in the modern realms of the Chaghadaids and the Golden Horde emerged as a result of the ethnic changes induced by the Mongols.

Mongol policies, especially the devastation that accompanied initial conquests, the mobilization of the army, the formation of new administrative divisions under the Mongol empire, the Mongol policy of ruling through foreigners, and, finally, imperial disintegration, which forced many new collectivities to refashion their identities, were crucial for the ethnic changes. These circumstances all led to the dispersion of many long-established steppe peoples (such as the Tanguts, the Uighurs, the Qipchaqs, and the Khitans) and to the emergence of new collectivities, which formed the basis for many of the modern Central Asian peoples (e.g., the Uzbeks and Kazakhs), as well as "pockets" of Muslims in contemporary Russia (such as the Tatars and Nogais). From the fourteenth century onward, most of the pre-Mongol steppe people were either assimilated into the sedentary civilizations surrounding them, mainly in China or Iran, or reduced to clan or tribal units in the new collectives established by the Mongols. The majority of these new ethnic formations coalesced after the collapse of the Mongol empire around the leadership of a certain Chinggisid prince (e.g. Özbeg, Nogay, Chaghadai and also – in the non-Chinggisid realm – 'Uthman). The name of the collective was not always identical to the name of its actual leader – in the case of the Uzbeks, the name only appeared several decades after the death of the Khan Özbeg, and became important only more than a hundred years after his death – but his supporters saw themselves as his *nökers* and named themselves after him. Most of these new groupings emerged in the Golden Horde realm during or after its dissolution, when the masses of Turco-Mongol people had already become Muslim. Thus Islam was an important component in the identity of these new collectivities. For instance, a major part of the appeal of Özbeg as an ancestor was the fact that he introduced Islam as the state religion of the Golden Horde. The degree of nomadism was also an important factor in the identity of these people, differentiating, for example, between the more settled Uzbeks and the nomadic Kazakhs. Most of the former steppe people, as well as some of the original Mongol tribes, remained as tribal or clan units within the new groupings. Thus we find Khitan, Qipchaq, Merkid, and Naiman among the tribes composing most of the modern Central Asian people. Yet, while there might have been some solidarity between the Uzbek Khitai tribe and the Kazakh Khitai tribe, for example, their main allegiance was to the new Chinggisid leadership of their post-Mongol collective, either Uzbek or Kazakh. In this respect, Chinggis Khan was second only to Stalin in reshaping the ethnic map of Central Asia.

THE LEGACY OF MONGOL STATECRAFT

Mongol institutional legacy varied in the various civilizations it affected. A more profound effect was felt in the regions where Mongol rule endured longer and where there was no strong indigenous tradition of a centralized state, namely in Central Asia and Russia. A certain institutional legacy, however, can also be discerned in China and Iran, and in the Muslim world the repercussions of Mongol influence reached beyond the limits of the empire. It is also worthwhile to differentiate between practical borrowing of Mongol institutions on the one hand, and adopting Mongol political ideology on the other.

The basic component of Mongol statecraft was the Chingissid principle: the notion that only descendants of Chinggis Khan were eligible to bear the title "khan," which denotes the highest political office. Although attempts to manipulate this principle began rather early (e.g., under Tamerlane), in Central Asia it remained valid until the late eighteenth century. The Chinggisid principle was relevant in other parts of the

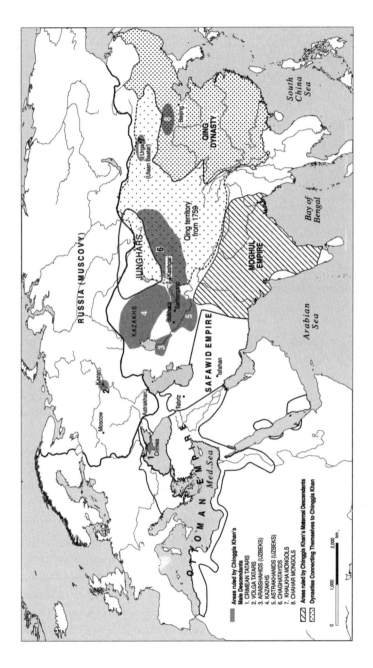

Map 5. Asia in the Mid-17th Century: The Chinggisid Legacy (with Qing expansion in the 18th Century)

Areas ruled by Chinggis Khan's
Male Descendants
1. CRIMEAN TATARS
2. VOLGA TATARS
3. ARABSHAHIDS (UZBEKS)
4. KAZAKHS
5. ASTRAKHANIDS (UZBEKS)
6. CHAGHATAYIDS
7. KHALKHA MONGOLS
8. CHAHAR MONGOLS

Areas ruled by Chinggis Khan's Maternal Descendants
Dynasties Connecting Themselves to Chinggis Khan

Muslim world as well, partly because the destruction of the Caliphate left a void in Muslim concepts of legitimation. The Moghuls in India, though emphasizing their Timurid genealogy, also made use of their Chinggisid connections as a legitimating element. Even in the Ottoman empire, where Chinggisid descent played no part in the rulers' identity, the Uzbeks and the Crimean Tatars enjoyed a special prestige due to their Chinggisid genealogy, and the sultans adopted the title Khaqan (originally Turkic but widely used in the pre-Ottoman period by the Mongol Great Khan). Even Muslim dynasties that deposed the Chinggisids (e.g., the Manghits in eighteenth-century Bukhara who replaced the Toqay-Timurid Uzbeks, the Kongrat who replaced the Arabshahids Uzbeks of Khiwa around the same time, or the Sufi Khwajas in eastern Turkestan who took the place of Moghulistan's Chaghadaids in the seventeenth century) stressed their maternal kinship to the Chinggisids or married Chinggisid princesses to bolster their (mostly Islamic) legitimation.

The Chinggisid principle also had an impact on Muscovy, where as late as 1575–6 Ivan the Terrible abdicated in favor of the Chinggisid Symon Bekbulatovich. It remained important to Russian politics until the westernization policies of Peter the Great in the late seventeenth and early eighteenth centuries. Yet even in the nineteenth century, Chinggisids living in the Russian empire demanded status as nobles on the basis of their genealogy. The Chinggisid tradition was also relevant in Qing China (1644–1911), where the ruling Manchus, after marrying Chinggisid princesses and obtaining the imperial seal from Chinggis's heirs, defined themselves as the successors of the Chinggisids. They used this status as one facet of their complex legitimation, which was particularly useful during their struggles with, and subjugation of, the Mongolian tribes (see chapter six).

In Central Asia adherence to the Chinggisid legacy was also expressed in the continued importance of the *Yasa* (Mongolian: *Jasaq*), the collection of laws ascribed to Chinggis Khan. Even after the Islamization of the Mongols in the fourteenth century the *Yasa* continued to be used together with Muslim law, the *Shariʿa*, despite several apparent contradictions between the two systems (such as the elevated position of Chinggis Khan among the *Yasa*'s adherents and the rules of ritual slaughter). These contradictions were highlighted by the Mamluks, who questioned the piety of the Ilkhans and Tamerlane alike for their supposed adherence to the *Yasa*. The contradictions sometimes embarrassed Central Asian rulers, too, such as Shahrukh, Tamerlane's son, who appears to have tried to abolish the *Yasa* but who could not eliminate its use. It certainly embarrassed the Central Asian Muslim clergy, who at times tried to Islamisize the ceremonies prescribed by the *Yasa*. For example, the felt carpet over which the newly-elected Uzbek khan, 'Abdallah, was supposed to be elevated as an important part of his enthronement in 1583, was washed in water from the Zamzam well in Mecca, thereby giving an Islamic touch to a Chinggisid pagan ritual. On the whole, however, the *Yasa* and the *Shariʿa* coexisted peacefully in Central Asia, each having its own sphere of application. The *Yasa* was particularly authoritative in political and criminal matters and in the realm of court ceremonies and protocol, while the *Shariʿa* prevailed mainly in matters dealing with cult, family law, personal status and contracts. The Muslim Central Asian khans and commanders who adhered to the *Yasa* certainly saw themselves as exemplary Muslims.

The *Yasa* was also important in other parts of the Muslim world. It remained valid in Moghul India, where it was often mentioned in order to highlight the rulers' links to Chinggis Khan and Tamerlane. Its practical use, however, seemed to have been confined to the realm of court ceremony and etiquette. The *Yasa* may have encouraged the promulgation of the Ottoman codex of "secular" law, the *Qanun*, and it also influenced Ottoman court etiquette. Even the Russians borrowed diplomatic practices from the Golden Horde, i.e., from the *Yasa* – a fact that was later to facilitate Russia's relations with Muslim dynasties, mainly the Ottomans.

Our partial knowledge of the Chinggisid *Yasa* of the thirteenth century makes it hard to establish how close Timurid or Uzbek laws were to the original *Yasa* (whatever that may have been; see chapter two). It seems, however, that in the post-Mongol world the *Yasa* – not unlike the Qur'an today – was used both as a concept that conveyed immense authority and was therefore invoked to legitimize policies, customs and regimes, and as a continuously evolving legal code. The *Yasa* legitimated different forms of government, both the relatively centralized regime of Tamerlane in the fourteenth to fifteenth centuries and the highly decentralized and tribalized rule of the Uzbeks in the sixteenth to eighteenth centuries. As a legal collection, some of the items ascribed to the *Yasa* in seventeenth-century

Central Asia, such as the status of the appanage of Balkh (in modern Afghanistan) as the seat of the heir apparent while the khan resided in Bukhara, were not a part of the *Yasa* even in the sixteenth century. Even more anachronistic is the claim by 'Abdallah Khan in the late sixteenth century that he performed the holiday prayers at the festival prayer grounds outside Bukhara according to the *Yasa* of Chinggis Khan. Indeed, when he captured Bukhara in 1221, Chinggis Khan went to these grounds, according to the thirteenth-century historian Juwayni, but he was not interested in praying. He had assembled the leaders of Bukhara there in order to confiscate their wealth. These anachronisms notwithstanding, many Central Asians (including Babur) believed that the *Yasa* perfectly reflected the situation during the time of Chinggis Khan, and the mere fact that such evolving laws and customs were sanctioned by Chinggis's name is significant enough. Ultimately, by the mid to late eighteenth century the authority of the *Yasa* had faded, but for five centuries it was the final arbiter of appropriate political behavior in Central Asia, where Chinggis Khan was second only to the Prophet Muhammad as a source of law and legitimation.

Borrowing of other elements of Mongol statecraft was of a more utilitarian nature. The Mongols developed efficient means to rule an empire and this fact was not overlooked by their successors. The Iranians (or the Chinese) did not need the Mongols to lay the foundations of an imperial system, but in Russia it was the example of the Golden Horde which was influential in turning a number of city states into the nucleus of a grand Eurasian empire, while Tamerlane's empire also owed much to Mongol precedents (of both the Chaghadaids and the Ilkhanids). Separate Mongol institutions were also retained in the different realms. Thus, for example, the Mongol post system continued to be used in Iran, as well as in China and Russia. The administrative division called *tümens,* originally formed to provide a Mongol military unit of 10,000 (*tümen*) with manpower or provisions, survived Mongol rule in Central Asia and Iran; a situation not unlike the survival of the Yuan system of provincial divisions (*sheng*) in Ming China. Iran and Central Asia retained the Mongol concept of landholding. The *soyurgal* (Mongolian: reward, hence appanage) replaced the Muslim *Iqta'* as a popular term for land holding and payment for officers. Unlike the classical *Iqta'* (discussed in chapter one), the *soyurgal* was hereditary and it granted its owner administrative and political rights over his appanage. Other Mongol financial institutions were influential in Iran, Central Asia, and Russia, where, for instance, the *tamgha* (custom tax) was retained even after the Islamization of the khanates, despite its un-Islamic character, and in general the taxation system of Iran into the Safawid period and of Timurid Central Asia preserved its Mongol features. In Iran, Central Asia, and Russia, the names of the currency –*tümen* in Iran, *kepek* and *den'ga* (or *tanga*) in Central Asia and Russia – go back to the Mongol period, suggestive of its role in the shaping of later currency systems. Mongol military institutions, eagerly adopted in both China and Russia, were less influential in the Muslim world due to the wide use of the alternative Mamluk system, which proved its superiority to (or at least its ability to cope with) the Mongols. In the long run, however, the advance of firearms, another technology the Mongols transferred across Eurasia, eventually marginalized the Mongol military legacy.

Clichés such as "if the Mongols had not burned Baghdad, the Muslims would have been the first to develop an atomic bomb" or other, more subtle attempts to ascribe the relative decline of the Islamic world vis-à-vis the West to the destruction wrought by Chinggis Khan and his heirs, are still heard today, especially in the Arab world. The reasons for the rise of the West and the "decline" of the East are far beyond the scope of this book, but certainly Chinggis Khan and his heirs bear little responsibility for this phenomenon. On the contrary, as this chapter has attempted to demonstrate, the Chinggisid legacy in the Muslim world was far from exclusively destructive. It included a long-lasting cultural effervescence, artistic and scientific exchange, booming international trade as well as new forms of legitimacy and law, considerable expansion of the world of Islam, and new groupings of Muslim peoples. Few of us would have liked to live under Chinggis's rule or even under his heirs', yet in retrospect Chinggis not only conquered the world, he also changed it. The same, often cruel, means which enabled a small nomadic minority to establish its rule over most of Eurasia, were also instrumental in creating conditions in which long-distance cultural and religious exchange flourished and new political culture and ethnic identities emerged.

The complex and long-lasting legacy of Chinggis Khan in the Muslim world is also expressed in his central place in the Muslim historiographical tradition, as will be discussed in the next chapter.

FROM THE ACCURSED TO THE REVERED FATHER AND BACK: CHANGING IMAGES OF CHINGGIS KHAN IN THE MUSLIM WORLD

The reason God wanted to elevate the might and glory of Chinggis Khan, his forefathers and ancestors, and his children and offspring and to raise the condition of that family was to strengthen the religion of Islam and propagate the law.

Rashid al-Din, (d. 1318); (Rashid/Thackston 1998–9: 1: 16)

You should know that from the beginning of the world and the creation of Adam and up to our days, there has been no Padshah, Sultan, Caliph, Caesar, Khan, Khaqan, Faghfur (emperor of China), Kisrā, Raja, Jipāl (king of Lahore), Porus (*Fūr*, a Raja slain by Alexander) and Tuba' (king of Yemen), *amīr* or king in the world who had more capacity for ruling than Chinggis Khan and his descendants.

Shabankarah'i, (d. 1357) 1986: 223

Chinggis Khan was a man of blood and fire. Directly he felt bored, he would remember the cities he had destroyed by fire, the men, women and children, the books, birds, cats, trees and grass he had wiped out; his boredom would then vanish and in place there would prevail a feeling of bliss that was like a solitary star twinkling in the nights of the earth's desert … He commanded the sun to set and its light to pale and, immediately and without hesitation, it obeyed.

Zakaria Tamer, (b. 1931) "The Day Genghis Khan Became Angry", in
Tamer 1985: 91, 94

Chinggis Khan's invasion of the Muslim world was highly dramatic, and not surprisingly most contemporary sources devoted a considerable amount of space to this event. The first depiction of Chinggis Khan in Muslim literature was as an arch enemy of Islam, often described as the "accursed" (*mal'ūn* or *la'īn*), and grisly descriptions of mass killing and destruction by his troops abound in both contemporary and later Muslim sources, including those written by subjects of his descendants. However, with the Islamization of the Mongols in Iran and later in southern Russia and Central Asia, and the incorporation of the Chinggisid principle (i.e. the notion that only Chinggis's descendants deserved to be rulers) into Muslim political culture, Chinggis Khan also became the revered father of, and a source of political legitimacy to, several Muslim dynasties in the Turco-Iranian world.

The endurance of Chinggisid rulers and concepts in the Muslim world meant that Chinggis did not vanish from the historical literature after the thirteenth century. On the contrary, like Alexander the Great (*Dhu al-Qarnayn*, "he with the two horns" in the Muslim tradition) or the Sasanid rulers of pre-Islamic Iran, Chinggis Khan became an integral part of Muslim history, even though he was not a Muslim. Sections devoted to Chinggis and his heirs appear in a large variety of Muslim literary genres from the thirteenth century onward, especially in universal histories[1] but also in many dynastic chronicles, geographical and administrative encyclopedias, religious literature, mirrors for princes, biographical dictionaries and, especially in Central Asia, in epic and popular literature.

Moreover, as in the case of the prophet Muhammad, there was a huge increase in "knowledge" about the hero after his death, and the political and religious needs of Chinggisid and even some non-Chinggisid rulers

[1] Muslim universal histories are compilations that begin with the creation, followed by a brief account of the prophets culminating with Muhammad, whose biography is followed by that of the first four caliphs. The rest will typically be divided into chapters for each Islamic dynasty more or less in a chronological order. A special place was usually reserved for the dynasty under which the work was written. The prototype of Muslim universal histories goes back to Arabic works such as Tabari's (d. 923), but for the Turco-Iranian world the main models were the Persian works of Rashid al-Din (d. 1318) and Mirkhwand (d. 1497).

therefore influenced the way Chinggis Khan was depicted in different Muslim contexts. Just like the changes of Muhammad's biography in the *hadith* literature, "new" episodes in Chinggis's biography reflected not so much the reality in his lifetime but the problems of the period in which his biography was written.

Apart from the political reworking, however, lots of new information about Chinggis, some of it originating in oral traditions, also found its way into the Muslim sources. This included, for example, the purported constellation of the stars during his birth (Chinggis was a Libra), and many fables and "words of wisdom" attributed to him. Some of those sayings were rather universal (not to say banal), such as those calling for respect for the law, the elders and the social hierarchy, or praising the value of a capable woman (Rashid/Thackston 1998–1999: 2: 296). Other anecdotes more closely reflected Chinggis's nomadic heritage, e.g., when Chinggis explains that his aim is to benefit his family and supporters:

> It is my sole purpose to make their mouths as sweet as sugar by favor, to bedeck them in garments spun with gold, to mount them upon fleet-footed steeds, to provide their animals with grassy meadows and to have all harmful brambles and thorns cleared from the roads and paths upon which they travel and not to allow weeds and thorns to grow in their pastures.
>
> Rashid/Thackston 1998–9:2:298

Another example is the story in which Chinggis Khan ordered the killing of the husband, brother and son of one woman because they had violated the *Yasa*. When the woman came to ask for his mercy, he allowed her to exempt one of the three. She chose the brother, explaining that she could have a new husband and a new son, but a brother was irreplaceable. Chinggis liked her reasoning and spared the life of all three. The most impressive aspect of this story (which could easily have been told of other rulers and periods) is the context in which it appears, in a late-fourteenth-century voluminous Mamluk work entitled *Tabaqat al-shafi'iyya al-kubra* (the comprehensive biographical dictionary of Shafi'i law scholars), a work dealing mainly with the biographies of scholars of one of the four legal schools in Sunni Islam. This was certainly not the most obvious place for a (highly constructed) biography of Chinggis Khan, yet the author, the Syrian scholar al-Subki (d. 1371), included it in his work, considering the Mongol invasion one of the major events of the times. In general, al-Subki followed the "accursed paradigm," describing Chinggis as a savage and the Mongol invasion as a huge tragedy for the world of Islam, but this particular anecdote was meant to illustrate Chinggis's unmatched wisdom, and so were others in his work (Subki 1964: 1: 331). Thus even those who cursed Chinggis were aware of his unique achievements and character. This certainly facilitated his later transformation from arch villain into revered father.

Since I cannot discuss all the Muslim literature on Chinggis Khan, stretching as it does over a vast area and nearly 800 years, I shall confine myself to analysing some examples of the changes in Chinggis's biography in the Muslim world, concentrating on two major themes related to his enduring political legacy. The first is the partial monotheisation of his figure, which was meant to overcome the problematic nature of using a pagan figure such as Chinggis as a source of legitimation. The process of "monotheisation" is apparent particularly around the time of Mongol conversion to Islam, the first half of the fourteenth century, although it continued to evolve afterwards, and most of the examples are taken either from the writing in the Ilkhanate (1260–1335) or in the Mamluk Sultanate (1250–1517).

The second theme highlights the function of Chinggis as progenitor of the political order. It examines those manipulations of Chinggis's biography which were meant to make it usable for legitimation of political and social orders quite different from his own. This began soon after his death, in order to legitimate the balance of power between the different Mongol branches, and continued to evolve, even among non-Chinggisid dynasties, as long as the Chinggisid principle remained valid, namely down to the nineteenth century. Chinggis's role as a source of legitimation, however, was limited to the Turco-Iranian world and was especially durable in the lands of Central Asia.

The last part of this chapter analyzes the image of Chinggis in the modern Muslim world, with examples from both the Arab world (mainly Egypt) and Central Asia. It argues that the change of political concepts in general, and the rise of the nation-state in particular, deprived the Chinggisid political legacy of most of its meaning and caused Chinggis Khan to be seen once again as the accursed conqueror and despot.

CHINGGIS THE MONOTHEIST

When the Mongols became Muslims, Chinggis came to be seen as the forefather of many Muslim dynasties. For the ideologues of the dynasties in question, this posed the problem of how to cope with the fact that Chinggis had inflicted more damage on the Muslim world than anyone before him and that he was, on top of that, an infidel; indeed, a pagan. Unlike the full appropriation of Chinggis in Tibetan Buddhism, adopted by his descendants in China and Mongolia (see chapter six), no Muslim source that I have read ever claimed that Chinggis was a Muslim. He was, however, depicted as a tool of God, thereby justifying his atrocities, and certain details of his biography were adjusted to better accommodate him to the monotheistic world order.

God's tool

Chinggis Khan's contemporaries (and not only in the Muslim world) tended to depict the Mongol invasion in apocalyptic terms. Thus the Muslims often connected it to traditions in which the infidel Turks invade the Muslim lands as part of the signs preceding the day of resurrection. The Sufi Najm al-Din Ghazi (d. 1256) even suggested a general explanation for the coming of the End of Days, namely that the reality of Islam had disappeared: its leaders only paid lip service to it and were not really devoted to it. Therefore God sent the unbelieving Tatars to overturn the "meaningless forms that remain" (Najm al-Din Razi 1982: 382–383; Lewisohn 1995: 57–58).

Since the End of Days did not arrive, however, other explanations for the Mongol invasion had to be found. Typically for a medieval society, pro-Mongol and anti-Mongol sources explained the coming of the Mongols as part of God's plan, a divine punishment: a view quite consistent with the way Chinggis and his heirs depicted themselves. The sins for which God chose to punish the Muslims by sending Chinggis Khan were usually connected to the Khwarazm Shah Muhammad, Chinggis Khan's main rival in the Muslim world. Several thirteenth-century sources imply that by enlarging his empire to the east (at the expense of the Qara Khitai) the Khwarazm Shah had breached the wall or dam separating the Abode of Islam from the wild eastern steppe, thereby bringing the Mongols into the Muslim world. Fourteenth-century sources are more explicit, describing the disaster brought about by the Mongols as a response to the Khwarazm Shah's killing of Chinggis Khan's (Muslim) traders in Utrar in 1218, or even to his execution of the Sufi Majd al-Din Baghdadi (d. 1219), who had been accused of having an affair with a noble Khwarazmian lady. In all cases, the cause seems rather too small in relation to the effect, perhaps because in the fourteenth century the evidence of the Mongol depredations was less visible than in the thirteenth century and could therefore be explained as originating in such specific actions. More importantly, identifying Mongol atrocities as God's will meant that they were rendered compatible with Chinggis's image as a revered father. The grisly descriptions of massacre and devastation were dutifully repeated in later Muslim sources, remaining one of Chinggis's trademarks, but they did not serve as an indictment any more. They did however allow adherents of the accursed paradigm to retain their negative view of the conqueror.

Moreover, in pro-Mongol sources Chinggis was depicted not only as God's punishment but as an integral part of a divine plan which in the long run meant to benefit the Muslims. Already, Juwayni (d. 1283, before the islamization of the Mongol khanates) had underscored the expansion of Islam under the Mongols, and their contribution to the Muslim world. He emphasized their liberation, in 1218, of the Muslims of Semirechye from the religious oppression of Güchülüg, the Naiman prince who took over the Qara Khitai empire, and finished his book with Hülegü's annihilation of the Assassins in 1256, a task which many Muslim rulers had attempted in vain to achieve, and which Juwayni compared to the Prophet's victory over the Jews of Khaybar. Trying to retain the Mongols' pro-Muslim image, Juwayni did not include in his book a description of the Mongol attack on the Abbasid Caliphate, an event which was harder to depict in a sympathetic light, even though as Hülegü's governor in Baghdad he had certainly had a first-hand knowledge of the episode.

After the Islamization of the Mongols, God's plan became clearer. Rashid al-Din (d. 1318) therefore presented a general framework for the reason behind Chinggis Khan's atrocities. As part of God's housekeeping of the world, He periodically chose "a great and mighty lord of fortune" who would cleanse the realm of the evil, corruption and decay which had emerged during the course of the passage of eons. God had chosen Chinggis Khan for this mission, and those who resisted him therefore also opposed God and were destroyed. When he finished cleansing the world, Chinggis created the imperial *Yasa* and *Yosun* (customs), spread justice, and nurtured his subjects. True, during the completion of the conquest of the world Chinggis caused much harm to Muslim urban areas, but as a balm for that, the people who inflicted such wounds to the Muslim world subsequently embraced Islam, thereby serving as a clear and obvious proof of the perfection of the divine power. The security and wealth of Iranian Muslims under the Muslim Ilkhan Ghazan (Rashid al-Din's patron, r. 1295–1304) and the strength of Islam under his reign (in terms of both converting the Mongols, Uighurs and sun worshippers and uprooting the polytheists and opponents of Islam) compensated for the misery Muslims had encountered at the hands of Chinggis Khan's troops. This view enabled Rashid al-Din explicitly to claim, as cited at the head of this chapter, that God's elevation of the Chinggisid family was actually meant to strengthen Islam (Rashid/Thackston 1998–9: 1: 16, 141–142). Later Sufi hagiographies describe a Muslim saint guiding Chinggis's forces in their invasion into the Muslim world, thereby stressing his role as God's tool.

Monotheisizing Chinggis's Biography

Chinggis Khan's religious functions in his own shamanic environment are well attested in Muslim (and other) sources. In post-islamization sources, however, there is a clear tendency to "monotheisize" those elements of Chinggis Khan's biography, although without ignoring their indigenous background.

A good example is the origins of Chinggis Khan. While the shamanic myth recalled in *The Secret History* ascribed the origin of the Mongols to the union of a blue wolf and a fallow doe, Rashid al-Din gave the Mongols a much longer ancestry originating in Japheth son of Noah, thereby locating them in a monotheistic genealogical framework, which was maintained in many subsequent Muslim works. Japheth was chosen because in Muslim tradition he was the father of the Turks, whom Rashid al-Din understood as closely related to the Mongols. He showed this again by creating a relationship between the Mongols and Oghuz Khan, the first Muslim Turk in Muslim tradition and the mythical forefather of the Seljuqs and later the Ottomans, a relationship which continued to evolve throughout the years.[2]

In connection with the direct ancestry of the Mongols, Rashid al-Din adduced another tradition: the Mongols once inhabited a valley called Ergene Qum, confined by impenetrable mountains and forests. After their number grew and the valley became too narrow for them, they broke out by melting an iron mine with bellows. The Mongol forefather who emerged from Ergene Qum was called Börte China (Blue Wolf); his wife was called Qo'ai Maral (White Doe), and all the Mongols were their descendants. Rashid al-Din thus recast the animal myth of the *Secret History*, depicting the direct forefathers of the Mongols not as wolf and doe, but rather as humans bearing animal names, thereby neutralizing its shamanic background. The Ergene Qum theme probably reflected an indigenous Mongolian tradition, though not one mentioned in the *Secret History*. It bears a striking similarity to the origin myths of the Turkic empire (sixth to eighth centuries), and was connected to the Mongols already by Juzjani, who wrote in Delhi in the 1260s and who ascribed the breaking of the wall to Chinggis himself. This connection was facilitated by the fact that Temüjin, Chinggis's original name, meant blacksmith. Muslim, Christian and Tangut (but not Mongol or Chinese) sources claimed he was a blacksmith, therefore skilled in melting iron walls. Several other versions of the story are retained in fourteenth-century Mamluk works, and it is often embellished with details originating in the Quranic story of Alexander imprisoning Gog and Magog, a barbarian nomadic people first mentioned in the Old Testament, behind an iron wall (Quran XVII:93–8; Ezekiel XXXVIII:39). It also surfaces in European sources on Mongol history, where it gathered details from the Syriac version of the Alexander

---

[2] The Mongols are described either as Oghuz's enemies (as in Rashid) or as his only surviving descendants (e.g. in Qazwini's *Ta'rikh-i Guzida*). The Ottomans tend to depict the Mongols as a lesser branch of the Oghuz and as later comers to Islam while the Uzbeks claim for Mongol priority, describing Oghuz as a descendant of Mongol Khan, father of the Mongols. See, e.g. Munajjim Bashi 1868: 1: 668–71; and Abu Ghazi 1970: 12–25.

Romance. In the context of monotheisization, however, the most striking feature appears in Qazwini's variant of the story. Hamdallah Mustawfi Qazwini, an Ilkhanid official and Rashid al-Din's disciple (d. ca. 1330s) describes the escape of the Mongol forefathers into Ergene Qum as *hijra*, giving it a status equal in importance to the prophet Muhammad's *hijra* which had begun the Islamic era. Immediately after this monotheistic statement, however, Qazwini mentions that at Ergene Qum the two Mongol forefathers (in his case the two surviving male descendants of Oghuz Khan: Kiyan, the progenitor of Chinggis's clan, the Kiyat; and Nökür) met a wolf, with whom they had descendants; but he adds that this tradition is "weak" (i.e. not well attested).

The amalgamation of monotheistic and shamanic elements in the stories of Chinggis's origin is best illustrated in the development of the story of Alan Qo'a, Chinggis's ancestress, whose miraculous impregnation is another obvious supernatural element in Chinggis's genealogy. According to the *Secret History*, after the death of her husband, Alan Qo'a was impregnated by a luminous being who left her tent disguised as a yellow dog. Already Rashid al-Din (and most of the subsequent Muslim literature) omits the dog, ascribing the impregnation to a more abstract luminous creature. Although he describes the story as a manifestation of divine power and defines "Alan Qo'a's pure womb" as the oyster shell for the precious pearl of Chinggis Khan's existence, Rashid al-Din remains skeptical about its credibility. In a further attempt to historicize the myth he tries to force it into a chronological framework, dating it either to the first part of the Abbasid Caliphate (established 750) or to Samanid times (819–1005). Fifteenth-century Timurid chronicles, however, already have exact dates: either 986–987 c.e. (376 according to the Hijri calendar), or in the times of Abu Muslim (d. 755), the maker of the Abbasid Revolution.

The story of Alan Qo'a was first compared to the virgin birth of Mary, mother of Jesus, the Maryam of the Quran, by the Mamluk official and encyclopedist, al-'Umari (d. 1348), who saw the Alan Qo'a version as a poor and implausible imitation of the Marian legend. For all that, both al-'Umari and other Mamluk sources, familiar with several versions of the story, conclude from the episode that Chinggis Khan was called "the son of the sun," a term that stresses his non-monotheistic connections. In Timurid and Moghul sources beginning with Yazdi (d. 1428), however, the Marian comparison is very much emphasized. It is adduced as a definite proof for the credibility of Alan Qo'a's story (and for her chastity). Alan Qo'a was impregnated by a ray of light that became a luminous shape inside her tent, just as Mary (Maryam) was impregnated by the angel Gibril (who blowed his breath into the fold of her shirt).

Another monotheistic context for Alan Qo'a's story is suggested by the inscriptions on Tamerlane's mausoleum in Samarqand, where his genealogy is given from Alan Qo'a downward (more about this below). After stressing that Alan Qo'a was not a prostitute, it explains that she was impregnated by a ray of light coming through the top of the tent, that took a human shape inside it "and it is said that he [the light turned into human] was one of the descendants of *amir al-mu'minin* 'Ali b. Abi Talib (Semonov 1948–1949: 57, cited in Aigle 2000: 154). The divine light which impregnated Alan Qo'a is therefore connected to God's hidden light emanating through Adam via the Prophet Muhammad into the family of 'Ali, Muhammad's cousin and son-in-law and the founder of Shi'ite Islam, thereby creating a connection between the families of Chinggis Khan, Tamerlane and the Prophet. While such a claim, so beneficial for Tamerlane's legitimation, was hard for most historians to accept, nonetheless it placed the Mongol shamanic myth in an Islamic framework.

The shamanic element was not completely eliminated, however, as is apparent in the *Daftar-Chingiz-namah* ("The Book of Chinggis's Legend"), an anonymous popular folkloristic Turkic work from the late seventeenth century which originated among the Volga Tatars, by then already under Russian rule. (Ivanics 2002 and forthcoming; Frank 1998:15–17). In this work, which traces Chinggis's genealogy from Japheth, son of Noah, Chinggis is a son of Alan Qo'a – a theme which has more in common with the Mary legend and which appears already in thirteenth-century Armenian sources – yet in the *Daftar*, the event is presented in a much more miraculous fashion than in earlier Muslim or Christian sources. Chinggis Khan's father, named Duyin Bayan ("Seed from God") was also a luminous creature. He too was conceived by a light beam which visited the daughter of Altan Khan, the Chinese (or

Jurchen) emperor, while she was locked in a stone palace. Sent away (by boat) due to her pregnancy, she found refuge among the Kiyat lineage and gave birth to Duyin. When he came of age, Duyin married Alan Qo'a, daughter of a Sultan related to Altan Khan. She gave him three sons, but Duyin did not think they were worthy of succeeding him. On his death bed he promised his followers that after his demise he would father a worthy son, who would be conceived when he, Duyin, would climb down as a light beam into Alan Qo'a's tent, leaving in the form of a wolf. His three sons duly stationed scouts near Alan Qo'a's tent after his death, and they saw a radiant sunshine descended from heaven that made them lose consciousness. When they awoke, they saw a bluish-grey wolf with a horse's mane coming out of the tent. He cried "Chinggis Chinggis," and disappeared in the forest. Alan Qo'a's son was therefore named Chinggis. He was born with golden diapers and with the seal of the prophet [sic] Gabriel on his shoulder. His shoulder blade resembled the back of a wolf and his beauty was like the beauty of Gabriel, leading everybody who caught sight of his face to declare he was ready to die for him (*Daftar*, in Ivanics, forthcoming, 1v–16v).

This tradition, certainly reflecting the Turkic-shamanic environment and giving such a prominent place to the wolf motive, has acquired some new monotheistic elements. These include the reference to Japheth as Chinggis's ancestor and the seal of Gabriel, reflecting the seal of prophethood that Muhammad had between his shoulders. In Muslim tradition, as mentioned above, Gabriel was God's messenger who was sent to impregnate Maryam and to announce to her the expected virgin birth. Thus the story might have also alluded to the Marian legend. In popular literature, as opposed to official chronicles, there was no need to eliminate the Turkic-shamanic layer, typical in later works of the Golden Horde.

The amalgamation of monotheistic and shamanic elements appears also with regard to Chinggis Khan's relations with the Divine. The steppe sky God, Tengri, was easily equated with Allah, yet Chinggis Khan's capacities as shaman are well attested in Muslim (and other) sources. In sources written after the Mongol conversion, however, there are at least two examples in which his shamanic capacities are combined with monotheistic features.

The first example appears in Shabankarah'i's description of the life of Chinggis Khan. Shabankarah'i (d. 1357), a Kurdish historian from southern Persia who wrote in the last decades of the Ilkhanate, and who usually follows Juwayni's account of Chinggis's life, stresses the close relationship between Chinggis and God: "Even though he was not a Muslim, he had true friendship with God", he claims (Shabankarah'i 1986: 227). According to him, Chinggis addressed God after the Utrar massacre, asking him to make him the ruler of the Muslims (*Tājīkān*), since he would have to attack them – despite his wish – due to the Khwarazm Shah's behavior. At the end of his address Chinggis raised his head from the ground and "they said he heard a voice saying: Go, because We will place them under your rule; We will give the whole world to you." When he came down from the hill, Chinggis began to make preparations to take his revenge on the Khwarazm Shah (Shabankarah'i 1986: 233–234.)

This paragraph certainly echoes the Mongol imperial ideology of world dominion conferred on Chinggis Khan and his descendants by heaven, but Shabankarah'i places it in a monotheistic context of a man speaking to God and hearing his voice replying to him, a description which brings to mind God's biblical promise to Abraham (Genesis 12:1–3). The friendship between Chinggis Khan and God also brings to mind the figure of Abraham, known in Arabic as God's friend (*al-khalīl*). It should also be mentioned that in the Muslim tradition Abraham was the first *ḥanif*, a term ascribed to an original monotheist (i.e. not yet Jewish, Christian or Muslim). It seems that while Chinggis could not be Islamized, post-conversion sources tried to "hanifize" him, thereby entering him into the monotheistic world order.

This is even more apparent in the second example, studied by Reuven Amitai. It appears in a Mamluk text, the universal encyclopedia of al-Nuwayri (d. 1333), though it probably originated in late Ilkhanid circles. According to this tradition, Chinggis Khan became an ascetic and isolated himself in the mountains. The reason for his asceticism was that he asked a Jew: "What gave Moses, Jesus and Muhammad their exalted position and spread their fame?" The Jew answered that they loved god and devoted themselves to him. When Chinggis Khan asked if the same means would work for him too, the Jew answered positively, adding that the Jewish books predicted that Chinggis Khan would have a victorious dynasty. Hence Chinggis Khan left his iron work and his family and became an ascetic in the mountains, eating only permissible food (*mubahat*). Nuwayri describes him dancing, spinning and receiving pilgrims who came to adore him. He adds that at the same time he did not obey any religion and did not belong to any religious community. He just had love for god, and this was the beginning of his rise (Nuwayri 1984: 27:302; Amitai, 2004).

This paragraph describes Chinggis Khan performing a complex shamanic ritual, and echoes the imperial ideology of the Mongols. Yet it also reflects a monotheistic context, because the role of the Jew as a harbinger of Chinggis Khan's greatness immediately brings to mind the role of the Jews and the Jewish scriptures as harbingers of Muhammad's prophecy (and Jesus' before him). By asking about Moses, Jesus and Muhammad, Chinggis Khan implicitly identifies himself as on a par with the great Muslim prophets (more about this below). The stress on eating the permitted food, in sharp contrast to early Muslim descriptions of Mongol diet, which includes pigs, dogs and blood, is also significant because the Mongol menu was often described as an important facet in their barbarianism and incompatibility with Muslim norms. Moreover, the term used (*mubahat*) has Sufi connotations: this is food left on the ground that poor sufis can gather and eat. Chinggis Khan's religious behavior as displayed in this episode therefore reflects a sort of Mongol "Hanifism," i.e. an undefined longing for monotheism before the adoption of Islam, nicely blended with his shamanic role.

Nuwayri's mention of Chinggis Khan along with Moses, Jesus and Muhammad brings us to the final theme, Muslim understanding of the reverence the Mongols showed for their forefather. Several Muslim sources equate Chinggis Khan to a prophet. While this certainly places him in a monotheistic context, it does so in a negative way since there is no prophet in Islam after Muhammad. The first treatment of Chinggis Khan as a prophet to the Mongols appears in the Mamluk work of Ibn Wasil (d. 1296, but wrote in 1260s), who connects this status to Chinggis Khan's being the source of Mongol law. The famous Syrian jurist Ibn Taymiyya (d. 1328) claims that the Mongols worshipped Chinggis Khan as a son of god, equated him to the prophet Muhammad and followed the "infidel shari'a" he conveyed out of his head. Ibn Taymiyya therefore does not accept the Muslim Ilkhans as true Muslims, accusing them of polytheism. Later Mamluk authorities simply claim that Chinggis Khan's followers obeyed him as the followers of the prophet obeyed the latter, or even as loyal slaves obey the Creator, thereby neutralizing the tension related to prophetic status. In Ilkhanid sources, the most peculiar reference to prophecy appears in the history of Wassaf (d. 1328), who tells the story of Sa'd al-Dawla, the Jewish *wazir* of the Ilkhan Arghun (1284–1291). Sa'd al-Dawla claimed that Arghun inherited the prophethood of Chinggis Khan and that he tried to establish a new religion on the eve of Mongol Islamization, planning to turn the Ka'ba in Mecca back into an idol temple. The mention of Gabriel as a prophet in the *Daftar* and the stress on Chinggis's beauty, a typical prophetic feature in Muslim tradition, suggests that on the popular level Chinggis remained connected to prophecy. Already in the late Ilkhanid period, however, Shabankarah'i makes this connection a positive one. After proclaiming that success such as that of Chinggis Khan must have originated in divine grace, he adds: "And if he (Chinggis) had been a Muslim, he would have partaken of prophecy and with his wisdom, escaped the tricks of fate (i.e. death)" (Shabankarah'i 1986: 223). The emphasis here is on Chinggis's intimacy with God, which had made him nearly equal in status to a prophet, and not on the prophethood.

In sum, by depicting Chinggis Khan as the tool of God, by partly monotheisizing the myths of his origin, and by synthesizing his shamanic indigenous functions with monotheistic "Hanifite" ones, pro-Mongol Muslim sources succeeded in making the Great Khan a highly honorable figure in the Turco-Persian Muslim collective memory, befitting his new position as the founding father of Muslim dynasties. Hints of his new role appeared even in the Arabic speaking world of the Mamluk sultanate. Some of the elements used by the pro-Mongol Muslim sources, however, could have been utilized also for retaining the accursed paradigm, which was more prevalent in the Arab world.

CHINGGIS AS PROGENITOR OF THE POLITICAL ORDER

If the attempts to monothesize Chinggis's biography were partly aimed at legitimating his position as a revered father of Muslim dynasties, the examples in this section illustrate changes in Chinggis's biography in which he was used to legitimate others – mainly later dynasties and leaders, both his descendants and others.

Already in the mid thirteenth century, Chinggis's authority was especially called upon to justify the outcome of the succession struggles among his descendants. He was therefore described as showing special favor to his younger son, Tolui, as part of the efforts of Tolui's son, Möngke (r. 1251–1259) to legitimize his seizure of the Qa'anate from the Ogödeids, descendants of Chinggis's successor. Later on, Chinggis's favor toward certain grandsons, such as Hülegü (r. 1260–1265), the founder of the Ilkhanate; Qubilai (r. 1260–1294), who established the Yuan dynasty in China or Shiban, Jochi's son and the ancestor of the Shaybanid Uzbeks, was emphasized by the historians of the relevant realms.

Chinggis was often also invoked to legitimate territorial divisions, which originated long after his time. Thus, for example, mid-fourteenth-century Iranian regional works portrayed Chinggis granting Tolui the right to rule in Iran, thereby justifying the rule of the Ilkhans there, a thorny point in Ilkhanid legitimacy because – unlike the rights of the Jochids or Chaghadaids – their right to Iran was not originally sanctioned by Chinggis. In a variant on this theme, the Mamluk author Ibn al-Dawadari (d. 1335) described Chinggis having a dream in which God explained to him that he had given him the world – apart from its western part (Egypt and North Africa), thereby predicting the future limits of Mongol rule in the Muslim world (and as a by-product giving Mamluk rule some pre-ordained glory).

More creative manipulations of Chinggis's biography were required for legitimating non-Chinggisid rulers. The best known examples come from Timurid histories, which provide an enormous amount of information on Chinggis's life. Tamerlane's connection with the Chinggisids was projected backwards into the period of both leaders' ancestors. The *Secret History* mentioned the Barulas, Tamerlane's tribe, as one of the many tribes which descended from Alan Qo'a, thereby giving him a common ancestress with Chinggis Khan. Timurid sources, beginning from Yazdi (d. 1428) who wrote under Tamerlane's son, Shahrukh (r. 1409–1447), not only stressed this common descent but also added an episode which allegedly took place in the generation in which

Chinggis's and Tamerlane's genealogies separated, that is between Tumanay Khan's twin sons, Qabul (Chinggis's great grandfather) and Qachulai (Tamerlane's forefather). One night Qachulai dreamt that he saw four stars rising successively from the breast of Qabul. The last of these stars filled the entire world with its brilliance, diffusing light to other bodies which sprang from the fourth star and continued to glow even after it had set. He then saw seven stars rising from his own breast, followed by an eighth star which cast its light everywhere and from which lesser bodies, each illuminating a different region, emanated. When he asked his father to interpret his dream, the latter explained that Qabul's descendant in the fourth generation – Chinggis Khan – would subjugate the world and divide it among his sons, while Qachulay's descendant of the eighth generation – Tamerlane – would also be a great conqueror, whose sons would share his glory. Tumanay Khan then asked his sons to take an oath in his presence that the khan's throne would belong to Qabul while Qachulay would hold the military and administrative authority. The oath, written in the Uighur script and sealed with a red seal, was deposited in the khan's treasury and later surfaced in Chinggis's time. The dream not only predicted later historical events, namely Tamerlane's rise to power, but also defined the later relationship between the Chinggisids and the Timurids (see chapter four). Interestingly, Abu al-Fadl, who retold the episode in the sixteenth-century *Akbar namah* (The Book of Akbar), written in India for the Moghul ruler Akbar (r. 1556–1605), Tamerlane's descendant, explained that Tumanay (or Yazdi) did not interpret well the dream: Qabul's star indeed referred to Chinggis, but Qachulay's eighth star was actually not Tamerlane but Akbar. Although there were fifteen generations between Qachulay and Akbar, only seven of them (that he did not specify) bore enough merit to be included among the series of stars, and Akbar was the eighth and most luminous one. (Woods 1990; Quinn 1998).

Another way of legitimizing Tamerlane through Chinggis's biography was the leading position of Qarachar, Tamerlane's ancestor who was a contemporary of Chinggis Khan. In thirteenth- and fourteenth-century sources Qarachar is barely mentioned, and all we know about him was that he was one of Chaghadai's commanders. In the Timurid sources, however, Qarachar appears in every important juncture in

Chinggis Khan dividing his empire among his sons, leaf from Rashid al-Din's *Jami' al-tawarikh*, Moghul India, reign of Akbar (1556–1605). The Metropolitan Museum of Art, Gift of Francis M. Weld, 1948 (48.144). *As an important source of legitimation, Chinggis is a very popular figure on Islamic illustrated manuscripts. Here, in an illustration from the reign of the great Moghul ruler Akbar Chinggis is depicted in a very Indian fashion*

Chinggis's life: he was among the first tribal leaders who submitted to him, he advised him throughout his career, and he was present in Baljuna, standing by Chinggis in his hardest trial and playing a pivotal role in the battle against Ong Khan. Qarachar also played a leading role on the eve of Chinggis's death when the latter reaffirmed his successor. In pre-Timurid sources this episode either was not mentioned or it was described as an informal gathering of Chinggis and his sons Tolui and Ögödei. In Timurid sources, however, the confirmation of the will is a solemn gathering, in which not only is Qarachar present, together with all of Chinggis's sons, but Chinggis praises his wisdom and advises his sons to follow his counsel. Chinggis then brings in the original covenant of Tumanay Khan, to which he appends an edict conferring the Qa'anate on Ögödei and entrusting Transoxania and the adjustment lands to Chaghadai. Entrusting Chaghadai to Qarachar, he orders his son to consider him his partner in rule and possession and never to disregard his advice, and appoints Qarachar to command Chaghaday's army and administration until Chinggis's death. Tamerlane's forefather therefore enjoyed the favor of Chinggis, who treated him almost like a son, and his special position in the Chaghadaid realm was sanctioned by Chinggis's last wish. No doubt this episode, repeated in Moghul but not in Uzbek sources, did much to enhance the legitimacy of Tamerlane and his descendents.

A similar use of Chinggis's biography appears in a nineteenth-century Chaghatay work, the *Firdaws al-iqbal* (Paradise of Good Fortune) of Shir Muhammad Munis, written in Khiwa between 1805 and 1842. This work, the largest historical work in post-classical Chaghatay, was commissioned by the first khan of the Qongrat (Mongolian: Qonggirad) dynasty, Eltüzer (r. 1804–1806), who after removing the Chinggisid puppet khan from Khwarazm proclaimed himself khan of Khiwa. Like Tamerlane, the Qongrats were non-Chinggisids who replaced the Chinggisids as actual rulers and in Eltüzer's case, also as the nominal rulers, bearing the title khan. Like Tamerlane, too, Eltüzer tried to prove the legitimacy of his dynasty through the special connections between his forefathers and Chinggis's family. Even in the *Secret History*, the Qonggirad (like the Barulas) and the Kiyat shared a common ancestry, and Mongol wives, including Chinggis Khan's Börte, were traditionally taken from them. Indeed

Munis stresses this fact; yet he also tries to show that the Qonggirad's tribal chief, Eltüzer's ancestor Tinim Güregen (Tinim, "the son-in-law," a title also borne by Tamerlane after he had married Chinggisid princesses) had held the highest position under Chinggis and his heirs, as Qarachar had done. Thus, the Qongirrad chief excelled in the battle against Jalal al-Din Khwarazm Shah just as Qarachar did against Ong Khan; and his subsequent appointment as a deputy of Jochi, Chinggis's eldest son and the ancestor of the Golden Horde and of the Chinggisid rulers of Khwarazm, mirrored the appointment of Qarachar in the Chaghadaid realm. Munis even brought in a parallel to the agreement between Qabul and Qachulai, although this was in the seventeenth century, long after Chinggis's time. (Bregel 1982, Bregel 1997).

The parallels between Munis's work and the Timurid chronicles attest to the continuing vitality of the Chinggisid tradition even in the early nineteenth century. Even after the Qongrat Khans, by then already settled, had deposed Chinggis's descendants, they still turned to Chinggis Khan to provide them with legitimacy.

The *Daftar Chingiz Nameh* develops a different perspective. Here Chinggis Khan is used to legitimate the tribal order of the Volga Tatars. The most striking feature of Chinggis's biography in the *Daftar* is its near complete disregard of Chinggis's campaigns both in the tribal arena and in the wider world. The changes in his biography here are thus much greater than in the Timurid or Qonggirad chronicles, which basically retained the thirteenth-century framework. In the *Daftar* Chinggis gains his leading position among the tribes not through his valor in battle but rather by impressing the tribal chiefs with his charisma (i.e., the unnatural circumstances of his birth, his unique beauty, and his attractive personality), causing them to invite him to be their leader – as was indeed the custom in the later Golden Horde. After he agreed to lead them, there is one sentence saying that Chinggis waged many wars and subdued many khans and hordes, but these are not described at all. Thus the devastation – the detailed descriptions of which appear in all the other sources mentioned above – is completely omitted. Instead we find Chinggis mostly hunting, yet his main function is to assert the relative position of the tribal leaders (*begs*) subject to him. To each of those who had invited him to rule, Chinggis assigns a specific *tamgha* (brand, seal), tree, bird, battle cry and later also body armor, all of which become the tribe's characteristic features. Chinggis's sons are mentioned in passing but obviously the tribal leaders are portrayed as much more important to the realm, a situation which also reflects the late Golden Horde reality. The role of the great conqueror in the *Daftar* is reserved for Tamerlane, who is described (in the work's next chapters) as the tool of God, fighting the infidel Russians and many others, and as an ideal Muslim ruler. Chinggis, on the other hand, is portrayed as the progenitor of the tribal political and social order. Other works of Central Asian popular literature of the eighteenth century, such as the *Chingiz namah*s (Books of Chinggis) prevailing in Central Asia or *Kunuz al-A'zam* (*The Great Treasures*, a legendary biography of Tamerlane), though often concentrating on local heroes – Tamerlane, Edigu (a Nogai amir) or Jochid khans – also reserved for Chinggis the position of either the ancestor or the creator of the political order. Obviously in the popular mind the rise of Chinggis Khan marked the beginning of a new era in Central Asian history, the repercussions and concepts of which were still apparent in the eighteenth and nineteenth centuries.

What we have seen so far illustrates Chinggis's prominent place in post-Mongol Muslim literary sources and some of the different uses of his biography. Chinggis's prominent place was particularly apparent in the Turco-Iranian world and in Central Asia. This was not only because of the longevity of his descendants' rule there but is also related to the prevailing types of historical writing: Chinggis retained an especially prominent position in realms in which universal histories were the common format (e.g. the Timurid realm) or where history was explained in terms of genealogy (e.g. Uzbek and post-Uzbek Central Asia). The shift from universal to strictly dynastic or regional histories led to a decrease in his prominence. Thus, for example, Safawid historiography in Iran, building on Timurid models, began with an upsurge of universal histories, but from the late seventeenth century it focused more on a dynastic history of the Safawids or on a history of the Shi'a (The Safawids were Twelver – or Imami – Shi'ites), thereby marginalizing the role given to non-Safawids or non-Shi'ite heroes, including Chinggis Khan. Another apparent case is Egypt. Whereas under the Mamluks in the thirteenth to fifteenth centuries we find a wealth of information about Chinggis Khan and the Mongols, and a highly universalistic approach to history, the Mongols are nearly completely absent from the historical sources of Ottoman Egypt (1517–1789), in which historical writing became local and provincial, just like the country itself. Even in the chronicle of al-Jabarti (1753–1826), by far the most noted historian of Ottoman Egypt, Chinggis is mentioned only as Hülegü's grandfather in the description of the battle of 'Ayn Jalut. The shift from universal histories to more local or to recent and contemporary ones is apparent also in the Ottoman Empire, especially from the eighteenth century onward, and in Moghul India from the seventeenth century. This historical shift also reflects the political framework, now more regional than universal. Yet it was the modern period with its new concepts of political identity that played the major role in marginalizing Chinggis in the Muslim world and in the revival of the accursed paradigm.

NATIONALISM AND THE MARGINALIZATION OF CHINGGIS IN THE MUSLIM WORLD

Chinggis Khan's enduring political legacy was the main reason for the reshaping of his biography and image in the Muslim world. The changing concepts of political identity in the modern world, mainly with the rise of national ideologies, thus led to his marginalization in the Muslim realm, while giving him a central place in other parts of the world, such as Mongolia and China (see chapter six). As territory and language replaced dynastic loyalty as major identity makers, Chinggis's position of the revered father was no longer meaningful in the Muslim world. By the new nationalist criteria, he was a complete outsider, a foreigner from far away Mongolia who did not speak any Muslim language, and who arrived as an invader. As Islam became part of the new national identity in most Muslim countries, Chinggis's unbelief also came to be (or more precisely remained) problematic. The nationalistic view of history adopted in most Muslim nations in the nineteenth and twentieth centuries therefore tended to present Chinggis as an outsider who wrought havoc and then vanished, his impact on the late-medieval Muslim world utterly denied. He returned to his position of the accursed enemy.

Nationalistic views of history apart, the renewed demonization of Chinggis was fuelled also by the fact that Muslim historians were gaining greater access to Occidental – Western European, Russian, Marxist – concepts of Chinggis Khan, which were particularly negative in the nineteenth and early twentieth centuries (see chapter six). The image of Chinggis as a cruel and barbarian oriental despot was easily supported by medieval Muslim sources, which stressed the great fear that Chinggis's subjects had for him, and was therefore highly appealing to modern Muslim historians.

The revival of the accursed paradigm and the modern appropriation of Chinggis took a somewhat different form in different Muslim contexts. I will focus on the Arab world (mainly Syria and Egypt) on the one hand, and Central Asia (mainly Uzbekistan and Kazakhstan) on the other.

By way of preliminaries, it should be noted that Chinggis's tyrannical image is found not just in historical, but also in literary works. The two Muslim accounts best known in the West to depict him as an arbitrary despot are those by the Syrian Zakaria Tamer (b. 1931) and the Kirgiz Chingiz Aitmatov (b. 1928). Tamer's short stories *Genghis Khan* and *The Day Genghis Khan Got Angry* (cited at the beginning of this chapter) were published in 1978, and can be read as an allegorical criticism of tyrannical rule in the contemporary Arab world. Aitmatov's famous novel *The Day Lasts More Than a Hundred Years* includes a legend about Chinggis Khan's white cloud, describing how the Great Khan lost Heaven's favor on his way to conquer Europe by enforcing inhuman laws such as prohibiting his subjects from having children till they had completed their conquest task. The beautiful legend, which includes many details and motives of the *Secret History*, depicts Chinggis as an arbitrary ruler of the Stalinist type, and indeed it was only added to the 1991 edition of the book (originally published in 1981), following the collapse of the Soviet Union.

Arab nationalism arose in the nineteenth century against the background of growing European interference and the Ottoman reforms. At first it was directed against Ottoman rule in the Arab lands, and the Mongols were grouped together with "the other" Turks (from the Abbasid Mamluks of the ninth century to the Ottomans) as those who bore responsibility for the Arab's (or Muslim's) lagging behind the west. The Mongols, however, held a special place among this group, since the rhetoric of Arab nationalism gave a prominent place to the fall of Baghdad in 1258. This was marked as the culmination of Arab weakness and the beginning of their dark age, in which they were politically dominated by non-Arabs. As the grandfather of the destroyer of Baghdad, Chinggis was portrayed as a barbarian savage who began the demolition of civilization which culminated in Hülegü's actions. Moreover, in most of the nationalistic histories (beginning with Jurji Zaydan's *Tarikh al-tamaddun al-islami* [History of Islamic Civilization] written between 1902 and 1905) the Mongols were excluded from the realm of Islam: they never managed to establish a long-lived state in the Muslim world and they never showed any interest in Muslim civilization, being merely lucky to arrive while it was already declining, mainly due to European attacks. Those writings also often completely ignored the Islamization of the Mongols, which would have made them insiders of Muslim, if not Arab, culture (Zaidan, 1902–1905:4: 204–212; see also Rifa'i 1970; Huwayri 1996; cf. Hasan 1954: 324–327).

Without the credit for the Islamization of his descendants, Chinggis remained only an outsider barbarian enemy. But even in that capacity, his importance was downgraded. In sharp contrast to medieval realities, the main rivals of the medieval Arab world (and of the Mamluks) in Arab national literature were not the Mongols but the Crusaders, the alleged forefathers of the western powers and later the Zionists. Thus one of the first examples of modern presentations of the history of the Arabs, *Durus al-tarikh al-arabi* (Lessons of Arab History) a textbook for secondary schools composed by Muhammad 'Izzat Darwazah (1887–1984), an Arab nationalist activist of Palestinian origin in the 1920s, mentioned the Tatars only in one sentence, as sealing the Caliphate's end, and completely ignored them in the section dealing with the Mamluks. The Crusaders' wars, on the other hand, are given a whole detailed chapter (Darwazah 1929; Choueiri, 2000; Haarman 2001). A certain exception to the neglect of the Mongol threat is the battle of 'Ayn Jalut, the most impressive Mamluk achievement against the Mongols. This is celebrated especially in Egyptian textbooks of the 1950s and 1960s as the battle which saved Egypt, the Muslim world, and Europe, from the barbarian Tatars; in the textbooks of the United Arab Republic (1958–1961) it even appears as a model of Egypto-Syrian cooperation.

Yet even these books gave more prominence to Mamluk battles against the Crusaders than to anti-Mongol campaigns. (See, for example, Amin Sa'id 1959: 8; Shihabi, 1965: 144–145; al-Qawsi 1966: 176–181.)

Recently, however, the Mongols came back to the frontline of the enemies of Arabs and Islam due to the American invasion of Iraq in 2003. The American siege on Baghdad invoked the memory of thirteenth-century atrocities. Accordingly, Arabic internet sites and articles compared George W. Bush with Hülegü, his brother Möngke and with Chinggis himself. A recent Egyptian popular history of the Mongols ("from their beginning to the battle of 'Ayn Jalut") devoted entire pages to a thorough comparison between the Mongols and the Americans, both, according to the pious Muslim writer, nations without history who paved their way to world leadership with heaps of skulls (Native Americans in the American case) and who have aspired to annihilate Islamic culture. Islam, as proven by the the 'Ain Jalut experience, will eventually be able to defeat its enemies if it revives its unity and its Jihadi spirit (Sargani 2006: 371–395). This new interest in the Mongols, however, is primarily because Chinggis and his heirs now have became relevant to the Arabs' conflict with the West, an asset which, unlike the Crusaders, they lacked until the American invasion of Baghdad. Needless to say, this new genre, stressing Chinggis's and his heir's anti-Islamic feelings as the main motive for their expansion, also completely ignores the Islamization of the Mongols.

The exclusion of Chinggis and his heirs from the Muslim world was easier in the Arabic speaking world than in the Turco-Iranian world, but there, too, modernism brought about the reconceptualization of Chinggis as the accursed despot. In twentieth-century Iran the Mongols, once a legitimate link in Iranian dynastic history, molded into both a Muslim appearance and a Pre-Islamic Persian one, became a synonym for huge devastation and traumatic alien conquest, which, however, failed to destroy Iranian culture. Although there are several solid Iranian studies of the Ilkhanid period (notably Abbas Iqbal's), the period does not loom large in modern Iranian historiography. In post-revolutionary histories of Iran, the Persian-speaking Jalal al-Din Khwarazm Shah, Chinggis's main rival in the Muslim world, is highly praised and more space is given to Iranian families active under the

Mongols than to the conquerors themselves. (e.g. Penahi 2002; Islam Niya, 2004; Navzari 2004; Mackey 1996: 71).

In Turkey the treatment of Chinggis is more ambivalent. While many Turkish children are still given his name, Chinggis is not included in the official Turkish pantheon, and his achievements, e.g. the *Yasa*, are ascribed to a Turkic tradition which had formed before him and upon which he built. The Mongols are treated (in continuation of Ottoman genealogies) as unsavory relatives, a marginal branch of the Turks, especially when compared to locals such as the Seljuqs or the Ottomans or even to the non-local Tamerlane, who was at least a good Muslim. (For example, *Türk Ansiklopedisi* 1964; q.v. Çingiz Han; Çingiz Yasasi; *The Turks* 2002, vol. 2; Pope 1997.)

In Central Asia, modern discourses of history and nation first appeared in the mid nineteenth century,[3] but the truly profound change occurred with the establishment of Soviet rule from 1917 and the enforcement of Stalin's concept of ethnic nationalism. Stalin defined ethno-national identity as composed of common language, territory, economy and psychological make-up, and the application of this concept to Soviet Central Asia resulted, in the 1920s to the 1930s, in the establishment of five republics: Uzbekistan, Kazakhstan, Tajikistan, Kirgizstan, and Turkmenistan. These newly established political entities were required to reassert their identities within their newly created boundaries according to Stalin's scheme, and the new identities were detrimental to the image of Chinggis Khan. First, Chinggis was once again an outsider in terms of language, territory, and religion;

[3] Apparent manifestation of these new concerns and the pan-Islamic trend which accompanied them appears in *al-Tawarikh al-bulghariyya*, a nineteenth century work attributed to Husam al-Din b. Sharf al-Din al-Bulghari. This work was composed in the same region in which the *Daftar* was compiled a century and a half beforehand, and became the most popular and widely read historical work among Volga Ural Muslim throughout the nineteenth and early twentieth centuries. In this work Chinggis portrayed as the infidel Khan of China, against whom the Muslim ruler, Tamerlane, sent his troops after Chinggis had refused to adopt Islam. Eventually Tamerlane kills Chinggis, thereby representing the victory of Islam. Here Chinggis is no more the progenitor of Muslim political order but an alien and infidel enemy. Frank 1998: 78–80.

second, as a nomad he represented a "primitive" stage of socio-political development in the Marxist scheme; third, as a putative enemy of the "Russian nation," which under Stalin's rule became the major source of loyalty for all Soviet citizens, he had no chance of historical clemency (see chapter six). Anti-Chinggis *topoi* were quickly disseminated from Russia into Central Asia, where the vilification of the Khan became even stronger than in the Arab world, since there were no Crusaders there to overshadow him. In the official histories of the Soviet Central Asian republics, therefore Chinggis was often depicted as a bloody barbarian tyrant who brought about not only notorious immediate destruction but also long-term stagnation to the history of the Asian nations.

The collapse of the Soviet Union opened a new period in the history and politics of the Central Asian republics. It did not bring, however, major improvement of Chinggis's image. In post-Soviet Central Asia territorial nationalism became much more powerfully pronounced than in the USSR era, and Chinggis therefore remained an outsider, unfit for the role of national hero, especially where local candidates were good enough. A comparison of Chinggis's position in Uzbekistan and Kazakhstan, both named after people long ruled by his descendants, is revealing of the impact of contemporary political needs on heroic past figures. In Uzbekistan Chinggis remained marginal since the country produced its own hero: Tamerlane. Unlike Chinggis, Tamerlane was not just local – his birthplace and his capital Samarqand are both inside the territory of modern Uzbekistan – but also Muslim, and so a much more appropriate national symbol. Moreover, Tamerlane had been a favorite hero of Central Asian popular literature from the eighteenth century onward and he was also a model of personal, authoritarian government well appreciated by Uzbekistan's president Karimov. He had left a visible and impressive legacy of monumental building and his "international" fame nearly equals that of Chinggis. Tamerlane therefore became the father of post-soviet Uzbekistan (even though the historical Uzbeks had driven his descendants out of Central Asia), and his sculptures replaced those of Lenin and Marx in the central squares of Tashkent and Samarqand. During this reconstruction of Tamerlane, his historical debt to Chinggisid concepts was completely forgotten.

Instead, Tamerlane is remembered as the one who defeated the Mongols, just as he did India, Russia, and the Ottomans.[4]

For the Kazakhs, who did not have a local hero of Tamerlane's caliber, Chinggis's place in the historical tradition is more ambivalent. On the one hand, Russian and Soviet influence has been much stronger in Kazakhstan than in Uzbekistan and the former negative attitudes toward Chinggis and the Mongols are still apparent. On the other hand, while Kazakh celebrities such as Ablai Khan (r. 1771–81), who led Kazakh opposition to the Zungars in the eighteenth century, adorn the Kazakh coinage, they are revered mainly by their descendants. What with the lack of commonly accepted national heroes, there are voices – mostly from the ranks of publicists and people from the technical sciences – who call for appropriating Chinggis. Chinggis's place, however, is not based on his position as the revered father of the Jochid princes who established the Kazakh union but rather on making him local, by claiming he was a Kazakh. The "Kazakhness" of Chinggis is based on the existence of tribes and clans bearing names of thirteenth-century Mongolian tribes in modern Kazakhstan, on genealogical manipulations, and on wild etymologies, which suggests that the names of Chinggis's forefathers were all Kazakh names. (Such absurd claims, for example the similarity between the names Yesügei and Issaq, have recently led a Ukrainian author to claim that Chinggis was a Jewish descendant of the Khazars [Zinukhov 2005].) Thus the Kazakh amateur historian Kalibek Daniiarov claims that the Kiyat, both Chinggis's clan and a tribe in modern Kazakhstan, was originally a Turkic, Kazakh tribe, descending from Oghuz Khan. The clan appears in the fifth to seventh centuries when the Kazakhs allegedly ruled the steppe. In the 970s the territory of Bodonchar, Alan Qo'a's son and Chinggis's ancestor, one of the leading Kiyat members, was located in the proto-Kazakh Kimek state in Kazakhstan. In the early thirteenth century the Kazakh Kiyat tribe was living on the borders of Mongolia, where the Kazakh Temüjin was born. Later he declared himself Chinggis Khan and returned to

---

[4] Moreover, in the region of medieval Khwarazm, now known as Khiwa or Qara Qalpakstan in northern Uzbekistan, the main local hero is Jalal al-Din Khwarazm Shah, whose fame rests mainly on his opposition to Chinggis. This further contributes to Chinggis's vilification in Uzbekistan.

conquer his homeland Kazakhstan. This speculation enabled Daniiarov to appropriate all of Chinggis's achievements for Kazakhstan, dismissing the claim that Chinggis was a Mongol as a mere myth (Daniiarov 1998: 175; 2001: 17–26, 349–362; http://www.washtimes.com/upi-breaking/ 20040406–123017–2002r.htm). The Kazakhness of Chinggis, however, is highly controversial even in Kazakhstan. Though it found a certain support among some nationalists in the new Kazakh upper and middle classes, professional Kazakh historians dismiss it completely and call for a more "scientific" evaluation of Chinggis's role in the shaping of the Kazakh identity, instead of depicting him as the sum of all evil or as the revered local father. (See, for example, Zardykhan in www.unesco.kz/ kazhistory/001_18.html.)

It is worth noting that the Kazakh Muslim minority in Mongolia had a completely different explanation for Chinggis's Kazakhness. According to this version (which goes back to medieval manipulations), Temüjin was not a member of the Kiyat tribe. He was not fathered by the Kiyat Yesügei, but was in fact the son of the Merkid to whom his mother was married before Yesügei had kidnapped her. Hence Chinggis was a Merkid, just like most of the Mongolian Kazakhs (Bulag 1994; Diener 2004).

In the post-Soviet world Chinggis has found supporters among some Muslim minorities in Russia, mainly the Tatars, heirs of the Volga Bulghars. With the end of communist indoctrination, Chinggis and the Golden Horde regained their heroic status and proved useful for constructing identities separate from that of the Russians. Thus, for example, the sixteenth-century Russian conquest of Kazan, currently the capital of Tatarstan, an autonomous republic inside Russia, had previously been celebrated as one of the great achievement of the expanding Russian empire, beneficial to all its ethnic groups, but in recent years it had become a day of mourning in Tatarastan. The day of the battle of Kulikovo in 1380, the first Russian victory over the Golden Horde, has been officially commemorated in Russia since 1995 as the day of victory of the Russian warriors over the Mongols-Tatars. In 2001, however, the council of Muftis of Russia issued a protest against this celebration, claiming that it does not contribute to the country's national unity. The stress in these views (which has not so far influenced the mainstream

Russian assessment: see chapter six) is more on the local heritage of the Golden Horde, but as a by-product Chinggis is slowly shifting once more from the accursed despot to the revered father.

Modern dilemmas and manipulations notwithstanding, one should not ignore the important and multi-faceted role of Chinggis in the pre-modern Muslim world. The infidel who devastated Muslim lands became God's intimate friend, the forefather of many Muslim dynasties, a source of legitimation for many others and the progenitor of the political and social order in Central Asia. It is hard to think of any other non-Muslim who won such prominence in the post-Muhammad world or who had received such extensive coverage in Muslim historical and epic literature. Chinggis Khan's unique career and enduring legacy certainly won him a place of honor both in Muslim literature and in the line of the makers of the Islamic world.

6

APPROPRIATING CHINGGIS:
A COMPARATIVE APPROACH

Born by the fate of the Supreme Tengri
From its beginning creating the supreme State
[Temüjin] caused all those of the world to enter his power
Temüjin became famous as the Great Chinggis Khan
[He] Brought the Five-colored Nations into his power
Set into order the state of the pleasant world
Invited kun-dga' snying-po, the Supreme Sa-skya Lama,
And was the first to propagate the religion of Buddha.

The Jewel Translucent Sutra (sixteenth century) (Elversklog 1999: 78)

This land so rich in beauty
Has made countless heroes bow in homage.
But alas! Qin Shihuang and han Wudi
Were lacking in literary grace
And Tang Taizong and Song Taizu
Had little poetry in their soul.
That proud son of Heaven, Genghis Khan
Knew only shooting eagles, bow outstretched.
All are past and gone!
For truly great men
Look to this age alone.

Mao Zedong, "Snow", 1945; http://en.chinabroadcast.cn/
1325/2003–12–26/90@72437.htm; Mao Tse-tung, 1959: 22, 36

Zingis Khan, whether we regard him as a conqueror or legislator, was, perhaps, the greatest prince that ever appeared in history. He not only secured the
empire of all Asia to his posterity for some ages, but even to this day two thirds
of that immense continent remains in the possession of princes of his blood ...
the Emperor of China, the Mogul of India, the great Chan of Tartary and the
princes of the Krim Tatars derive their blood from Zingis; and it is remarkable
that at one period there were five hundred crowned heads of his race in Asia.

> From the advertisement to Alexander Daw's tragedy *Zingis*,
> presented at Drury Lane theatre, London, 1768; Daw 1769: 1

Chinggis Khan was a maker of the Muslim world, but he has also maintained a strategic position in the making and imagination of other parts
of the world. This last chapter reviews the development of Chinggis's
image in Mongolia and China and more briefly his position in Russia and
the West, thereby providing a comparative framework in which to view
Chinggis's fate in the Muslim world. In the non-Muslim realms Chinggis
remains a powerful political symbol, often with strong religious and
cultural overtones, and there too his image shifts between the poles of a
super hero and an arch enemy.

MONGOLIA

Given his continuing importance in the post-Chinggisid Muslim world, it
is somewhat surprising that the Great Khan did not always retain his political prominence in his homeland. In 1368 when Chinggis's heirs, Yuan
dynasty rulers, were overthrown by the ethnic-Chinese Ming dynasty
and driven from Beijing to Qara Qorum, Chinggis's name was not sufficient to keep the Mongols united. The political framework in Mongolia,
a series of rival confederations competing for power, prevailed until the
eighteenth century when Qing China, led by the Manchus, took over
Mongolia. The Chinggisid principle was challenged in Mongolia, whereas
it was preserved in the Muslim world. True, Chinggis's direct descendants, known as the Golden family, continued to adhere to it as well as
practicing the Chinggis Khan cult based on Yuan precedents, and they
usually headed at least one of the tribal confederations of Mongolia. Yet

their Chinggisid claim was insufficient to assert a leading position in Mongolia nor was it enough to unite the feuding tribes.

In the late sixteenth century, the search for a broader common ground led Altan Khan, the Chinggisid leader of the Tümed confederation in Mongolia, to adopt Tibetan Buddhism – thereby creating the famous title Dalai Lama, the Oceanic Lama, as he called the Tibetan priest who converted him. The Mongols had adhered to Tibetan Buddhism when they ruled in China, but abandoned it after the fall of the Yuan. Reintroduced to Mongolia by the Chinggisid Altan Khan, Tibetan Buddhism in Mongolia was quick to incorporate Chinggis, giving him a central place in its cult and imagery. Since, unlike Islam, Buddhism is not an exclusive religion, Chinggis's shamanic role was not an obstacle to such inclusion. In sixteenth-century Mongolia, as in Yuan times, Chinggis was defined as an incarnation of the ancient Chakravartin, the universal ruler who turned the wheel of the Buddhist Law (*Dharma*), modeled after the Indian king Ashoka; but now he was also connected genealogically to the ancient kings of Tibet and India, and later to the Buddha himself. He was also portrayed as the incarnation of the bodhisattva Vajrabani ("holder of the thunderbolt," one of the more martial figures in the Buddhist pantheon deriving from the Indian god of thunder). Due to the quick spread of Tibetan Buddhism in Mongolia from the sixteenth century onward, the Buddhist incorporation of Chinggis Khan contributed significantly to his popularization as a symbol not only among his noble descendants but also among Mongol commoners. It is also in this period that we find Chinggis described as the founder of many of Mongolia's customs, from marriage ceremonies to the best way of treating horses.

The conversion to Buddhism also inaugurated a period of literary renaissance in Mongolia, where it flourished in the seventeenth and eighteenth centuries, before and during Manchu rule. Many epic chronicles, most of them with a strong Buddhist flavor, were composed in this period and many dealt with the Mongol golden past. In this literature, Chinggis's biography went through significant changes in order to make him better suited for his new Buddhist role. The manipulation of the inherited Mongol tradition seen here makes that attested to in the Muslim world seem quite negligible. The ancestors of the Mongols – the

Blue Wolf and Fallow Doe of the *Secret History* – were personalized (just like they were in Rashid al-Din's work), and described as descendants of the Tibetan and Indian kings who arrived in Mongolia from Tibet; Alan Qo'a was impregnated by the Lord of High Qormuzda, an important deity in the Buddhist pantheon, thereby making Chinggis a son of God. Chinggis's birth was ordained by the Buddha; Chinggis was born not with a clot of blood but with a seal – the symbol of political leadership, not of violence; Chinggis was the first to propagate the religion of Buddha in Mongolia and the one who invited from Tibet the supreme Sa-Skya lama (summoned by Chinggis's grandson, Qubilai, in thirteenth-century works), allegedly giving him the final religious authority while retaining political authority for himself. Chinggis's wars were meant to save the world from evil kings and many of his battles became scenes of miraculous combats won by supernatural skills. Thus, for example, Chinggis's last battle with the Tanguts was described as a personal combat between Chinggis and the Tangut ruler, decided by shape-shifting: the Tangut monarch transformed himself into a snake, but Chinggis turned into a *Karaudi*, the king of all birds; the Tangut ruler was then transformed into a tiger, but Chinggis became a lion, king of all beasts. Finally the Tangut khan was transformed into a boy; Chinggis then turned into Qormuzda, the Lord of High, and the Tangut was exhausted and captured (Sayang Sehen, *Erdeni-yin Tobchi*, cited in Jagchid 1988: 302). The "total war" of the Mongols was therefore turned into a series of magical confrontations rich in folkloristic details, but omitting both its strategic and military uniqueness and the devastation it caused.

Even Buddhism, however, was not enough to unite the Mongols, and their lack of unity, as well as Manchu manipulation of the symbol of Chinggis (discussed below), were among the main reasons for the Qing takeover of Mongolia. This took place in different stages, from the incorporation of the Chahar Mongols, Chinggis's descendants who populated southern Mongolia, later known as Inner Mongolia, in 1634, to the inclusion of the Khalkha confederation of northern or Outer Mongolia in 1691 and the massacre of the Zunghars (or Oyirads) in western Mongolia in the mid-eighteenth century. During this period there were several attempts – mainly led by the non-Chinggisid Zunghars – to invoke the theme of pan-Mongolian unity, but none of them succeeded. Another, initiated by one of the Khalkha Khans after the Qing had incorporated the Chahar Mongols, involved the selection of a *Bogdo Gegen*, a living Buddha, a Mongol boy who would be the reincarnation of earlier great religious figures. The *Bogdo Gegen* was meant to emancipate the Mongols from their submission to Tibetan priests and to become a symbol which would facilitate Mongol unification, both religiously and politically. The first *Bogdo Gegen*, selected in the late 1630s, won popularity and prestige in the religious sphere, but he was less successful politically, being too closely identified with the khan who appointed him. In 1757, a Chinggisid was chosen to be the new *Bogdo Gegen* after a Khalkha rebellion. The fact that he was a Chingisid improved his chances of combining political and religious legitimacy. In its capacity as the Khalkha's overlord the Manchu-Qing government therefore decreed that later reincarnations should no longer be sought in Mongolia, but only in Tibet, which by then was under firm Manchu control. Later, the Qing fostered an expansion in the number of the incarnations, thereby further fragmenting the *Bogdo Gegen*'s authority.

Manchu colonial rule, however, inadvertently contributed to the resurgence of Mongol unity. While they appropriated Chinggis and the cultural capital that accompanied him, the Manchus undermined the traditional leadership and lifestyle in Mongolia in order to facilitate their rule. They created new administrative divisions, which cut through the established khanates and limited the seasonal migration routes. This, combined with the need to finance Qing bureaucratic apparatus in Mongolia, contributed to the country's impoverishment. Concomitantly, Qing encouragement of the further spread of Buddhist monasteries created a situation in which, by the mid-nineteenth century, about forty percent of the males in Outer Mongolia were monks, contributing to demographic decline in this sparsely-populated region.

This deteriorating economic situation created opportunities for the penetration of Russian and Chinese merchants' into Mongolia, despite the Manchu's initial attempts to isolate this country from its neighbors. In the nineteenth century, when the Manchus, facing a huge population growth in China and occupied on other fronts, revoked the isolation policy, a vast Chinese colonization of Mongolia began. This led not only to the increasing interaction between Mongols and Chinese but also to the further decline of the Mongols' socio-political status and their loss of choice pasturelands to the incoming Chinese. The increasing tension with the Chinese immigrants, and the impact of national ideas arriving from Russia, contributed to the emergence of a new Mongolian national identity, directed primarily against the Chinese.

For Mongol nationalism, Chinggis Khan, the most famous native son, its great unifier who had subdued parts of both China and Russia, was of course the obvious choice for a national hero. Thus, more than six hundred years after his death Chinggis transformed, in Almaz Khan words, from imperial ancestor of his Golden Family to an ethnic hero and national symbol of all the Mongols (Khan 1995: 248). Aside from retaining his divine status and his position as culture founder, Chinggis was again hailed as a political symbol, a great conqueror who had led the unified Mongolians to international fame. His new role found expression, for example, in the first Mongol historical novel, *The Blue Chronicle (Köke sudur)* published in 1871 by Injannasi, a descendant of Chinggis of the twenty-eighth generation from Inner Mongolia. The novel reports Chinggis's biography according to the *Secret History* and Chinese sources, and presents Chinggis and his companions as realistic – even if larger than life – heroes, not as Buddhist saints. It also introduces many fictional secondary characters, whose romantic adventures add much to the work's appeal (Hangin 1973).

The nascent Mongolian national movement did not manage to free Inner Mongolia from Chinese rule, but it did succeed in securing the autonomy of Outer Mongolia after the Manchu-Qing dynasty fell in 1911 – the only part of Qing conquered territories which remained outside China's control. In 1911 Mongolia became a theocracy led by the *Bodgo Gegen*, and Buddhism, not nationalism, remained the main cement bonding the Mongols. Yet Mongolia's autonomy was only achieved by Russian and later Soviet support. Mongolia was swiftly engulfed in the Russian civil war, which brought about the 1921 revolution, when the Soviet Red Army, allegedly checking China's attempts to retake Mongolia, established a pro-Soviet government under the nominal rule of the restored *Bodgo Gegen*. With his death in 1924 Mongolia became the People's Republic of Mongolia, a Soviet satellite.

Under the Communist regime, the Mongols were not allowed to use their national symbol, Chinggis Khan. In a way similar to his fate in Soviet

Central Asia, under the dominating Soviet narrative Chinggis was reinterpreted as an enemy of mankind even in his homeland. In the 1930s to 1940s Chinggis's name became virtually taboo in Mongolia. Both Buddhism and the Chinggis Khan cult were repressed; the Cyrillic alphabet replaced the script that Chinggis had chosen for his people in 1204; and historians who had tried to portray Chinggis in a positive light were dismissed and exiled. Instead, modern heroes such as Sühebaatar (1893–1923), the leader of the 1921 revolution; Choibalsan, the Mongolian prime-minister (1936–1952); and his friend and model, Joseph Stalin, were glorified in Mongolia. *The History of the People's Republic of Mongolia*, which was published in 1954 in Mongolian and Russian, referred to the period of Chinggis Khan as a reactionary, backward and feudal age. Yet even in the official Socialist writing, Chinggis's vilification was not complete. The feudal oppressor of the masses was grudgingly accorded recognition for the creation of the Mongolian state and thus for providing impetus for social development. His campaigns of conquest and the massacres which accompanied them, however, created obstacles for further social development, therefore defining his reign as reactionary. Moreover, the official Socialist historiography, due to its stress on the national character of the People's Republic of Mongolia, paradoxically strengthened the political dimension of Chinggis's figure as opposed to the religious and folkloristic ones. Official propaganda notwithstanding, however, Chinggis retained much of his reputation on the popular level. Chinggis's popularity was manifested in the huge celebrations planned on the occasion of Chinggis's 800th birthday in 1962. However, despite the relaxation of the political climate in the post-Stalin U.S.S.R. and its satellites, the celebrations were canceled at the last moment, either on Moscow's orders or under the direction of the alarmed Mongolian Communist Party, and their organizers were imprisoned.

The relaxation of communist indoctrination in Mongolia since the 1970s and especially under the *glasnost* of the 1980s has led to a gradual recovery of Chinggis's position. This tendency has reached new heights since the fall of the Soviet Union in 1991 and the new – and this time real – independence of Mongolia. Post-1991 Mongolia has embraced Chinggis as its national symbol without restraint. He appears on coinage and postage and it seems as if nearly everything – from Ulaanbataar's

Mongolian Stamps Commemorating the 750th anniversary of
the *Secret History of the Mongols*, 1990

international airport to different brands of alcohol – is named after him.
More surprising, the same Chinggis who was depicted as a barbarian
and reactionary tyrant is now playing a leading role in Mongolia's peace-
ful – and highly praised – transition from communism to democracy.
Modern Mongolians stress Chinggis's role as creator of a united Mongol
state – his political and civil legacy – as opposed to his military one.
Chinggis's conquests are described as a mere "product of their time"
which suffices for explaining the cruelty and devastation that accompanied them. In contrast, his policies are said to have set the stage for con-
sultative institutions (the *Quriltai*, the inspiration for the name of the
contemporary Mongol parliament, Hural) and participatory government, the rule of law, independent judiciary and equality before the law
(the *Yasa /Jasaq*) and even human rights (Enkhtuvshin and Tsolmon
2003). In fact, some western researchers also attribute the quick shift
from communism to democracy to Mongolia's nomadic political culture, which goes back to Chinggis Khan (Sabloff 2002). Contemporary

Mongols also stress Chinggis's universal importance, and his significant contribution to economic and cultural exchange between East and West, and many international activities are planned for the celebration of the 800th anniversary of the 1206 *quriltai* in 2006. Currently the Mongols also take pride in the growing popularity of their national hero in other parts of the world, mainly China and the West.

CHINA

The Mongols only conquered parts of the Muslim world, but they conquered the whole of China, their conquest being the first time that the whole Middle Kingdom fell into foreign hands. But while in certain periods Mongol rule did indeed exemplify traumatic barbarian conquest for the Chinese, the appropriation of the Mongols there began earlier than in the Muslim world and was much more complete. Moreover, due to the firm incorporation of Inner Mongolia, the most populated part of Chinggis's homeland, into the Chinese polity beginning in the seventeenth century, and further, since more Mongols now live in China than in Mongolia, Chinggis remained a highly relevant symbol in modern China. In contrast to his lot in the contemporary Muslim world, Chinggis is currently one of China's most celebrated national heroes.

In 1263 Chinggis posthumously acquired an imperial status in China. On the eve of the establishment of the Yuan dynasty and the final conquest of southern China, Chinggis's grandson, Qubilai Khan, declared himself a Chinese emperor and conferred on his grandfather the title of *Taizu*, the "Supreme Ancestor." Chinggis therefore became the revered father of the Yuan dynasty, and was placed at the apex of the Chinese world order, as the recipient of the Heavenly Mandate, which enabled him to found a dynasty. His unprecedented conquests and Qubilai's eventual reunification of China were interpreted as definite proof of his firm hold on the mandate. Moreover, Chinggis's political prominence was reinforced by religious belief and practice: Yuan emperors, following steppe traditions of ancestor worship, performed a special ancestral cult for Chinggis Khan and, with the adoption of Buddhism, also declared him an incarnation of Chakravartin (the king who turns the wheel of the Buddhist law), a position he later re-assumed in Mongolia, as mentioned above.

The Ming dynasty which succeeded the Yuan in 1368 preserved Chinggis's position as the Yuan founding father, and even the Ming founder himself affirmed the validity of Chinggis's mandate. The first chapter of the *Yuan shi* (the official Yuan history), written under the Ming in 1370, begins with Chinggis's ancestors (commencing with Alan Qo'a's miraculous impregnation by light and the subsequent birth of Bodonchar, the wolves and other animals excluded) and ends with Chinggis's death. It retains Chinggis's Buddhist titles, but stresses his military genius. The chapter is, however, very laconic in the description of the conquests, and mostly ignores the devastation which accompanied them. It also gives more space to the events in China than to the western campaign. This Sinocentric point of view generally characterizes the *Yuan shi*, which barely acknowledges the Eurasian facet of the Yuan dynasty and gives only sporadic details on the other Mongol khanates. As a result, the Ming authors of the *Yuan shi*, while preserving Chinggis's position as the dynasty's founder, also belittled his career, placing him in the same category as that of the founders of the Liao or Jin dynasties: a non-Chinese who established a Chinese-like dynasty that ruled for a relatively short period, serving most importantly as a precursor to the Ming.

In the late Ming, however, after a series of defeats that the Mongols inflicted on the Chinese (and which led among others to the construction of the so-called Great Wall of China), the Yuan was conceived differently. While still retaining its legitimate dynastic status, the Yuan was reinterpreted by many scholars as a traumatic experience, a historical aberration, when China was ruled by foreign barbarians instead of ruling them. Moreover, insofar as Yuan inherited the mandate of the Song dynasty (960–1279), this meant that its true history should begin with Qubilai, who conquered the Song, and not with Chinggis, who was henceforth increasingly marginalized.

Chinggis came back into the limelight in China when it was once more conquered from Inner Asia, this time by the Manchus, heirs of the thirteenth-century Jurchens, who overthrew the Ming and established the Qing dynasty (1644–1911). The Manchus had spent much of their predynastic period in close proximity to the Mongols, and borrowed from them most of their political culture, including the Chinggisid principle. After subduing the Mongol Chahars, Chinggis's direct descendants, in 1634, the Manchus appropriated their symbols of authority, such as the Chinggisid seal and the cult of Chinggis Khan. Like Tamerlane and other non-Chinggisid rulers in the Muslim world, the Manchus married Chinggisid princesses and portrayed themselves as Chinggis's legitimate heirs. Moreover, the Manchus also adopted Tibetan Buddhism and were therefore able to fashion another type of bond with Chinggis. The Manchu fore-fathers, Nurgachi (d. 1626) and Hong Taiji (d. 1643), presented themselves as Buddhist incarnations of Chinggis and Qubilai, and these positions were continuously held by later Manchu emperors ruling from Beijing.

Building on their religious and genealogical (if only marital) connection to Chinggis, the Manchu portrayed themselves as Chinggis's true heirs, employing the Chinggisid principle as one facet of their complex legitimacy, in a way reminiscent of its use by Muslim rulers of Chinggisid descent. This appropriation proved successful: in 1691 the Manchus, relying also on their military might, managed to convince the Khalkha Mongols to support the "Chinggisid" Manchus against the non-Chinggisid Western Mongols, the Zunghars (Oyrats). With the Khalkha's help the Manchus eventually managed to triumph over the Zunghars, thereby achieving what many Chinese dynasties attempted to do in vain throughout history – subdue the nomads of Mongolia. The Mongols became part of the five peoples who made up the bulk of the subjects of the Qing dynasty, the others being the Manchus, the Chinese, the Tibetans and the Muslims.

For the Manchus, Chinggis was useful not only for ruling the Mongols but also for governing their Chinese subjects. From the beginning of their imperial enterprise, Nurgachi and Hong Taiji showed great interest in the history of the foreign conquerors of China who had preceded them, especially the most successful ones – the Mongols, whom they saw as a source of historical lessons which would facilitate their own future conquest and rule of China. In 1644, on the eve of the Manchu's entry into Beijing, the official histories of the Liao, Jin and Yuan were translated into Manchu. In the historical precedents which the Manchus cited in their internal and external correspondence in the first half of the seventeenth century, they gave the place of honor to

Chinggis Khan as the ultimate example of a foreigner who had held the mandate of heaven in the Middle Kingdom.

The continued interest of the Manchus in the history of China's foreign dynasties also led to a large increase in the historical study of the Yuan in Qing China. This was mainly the work of Chinese scholars, who, while frequently focusing on the role of Chinese literati under Mongol rule, also studied the history of the Mongol themselves. Since Chinggis's biography was part of Yuan history, it was routinely included in general histor-ies of China compiled under the Qing and in the more specific studies devoted to the Mongols, which combined information from the *Secret History* with that of Yuan private histories, memoirs and inscriptions.

In the nineteenth century this field was given a boost by the discovery of Muslim sources on the Mongols. The discovery was made mainly by Chinese diplomats who gained second or third hand access to Muslim sources on the Mongols while serving in Europe. Pleased to find common historical ground between China and the West, they translated parts of these sources into Chinese and the extracts were incorporated into later works on Yuan history.[1] This enabled the Chinese to broaden their knowledge on Chinggis and to give more space to his western campaigns. The *XinYuan shi* (the new official history of the Yuan), a culmination of Qing efforts, published only under the Chinese republic in 1922, included one chapter on Mongol origins and two chapters on Chinggis's reign (until 1206 and afterwards). The vicissitudes of Chinggis's conquests received more space in the *XinYuan shi*, yet as dynastic founder he still enjoyed a positive historical assessment.

The intense Chinese nationalism of the early twentieth century, initially directed against the Manchus but hostile to any non-Chinese

[1] The pioneering work was Hong Jun's *Yuan shi yiwen zhengbu jiaozhu* (An Annotated Edition of Translated Supplements to Yuan History). Hong (1840–93), a Chinese diplomat who had served in Berlin and St. Petersburg, translated a collection of passages mainly from the translation of Rashid al-Din's work and from D'Ohsson's multi-volume work (published 1834–35) on the Mongols (see below) commenting on their relation to Yuan history. His work was a source for major Chinese compilations such as Tu Ji's (1856–1921) *Mengguer shiji* (Historical Records on the Mongols) and Ke Shaomin's (1850–1933) *Xin Yuanshi* (the new official history of the Yuan).

domination, caused the Mongol conquest and the Yuan period once again to be perceived as a trauma to the Chinese, and later to serve as a popular analogy for the Japanese occupation of the 1930s to 1940s. The very right of the Yuan to rule was questioned, and some historians even suggested that it should be deleted from the Chinese dynastic circle, which should pass directly from the Song dynasty to the Ming.

Ironically, however, at the very time when he was being ousted from his position as Chinese emperor, Chinggis regained his position as a useful political symbol in China. This was because in the early twentieth century Chinese nationalists were trying hard "to pull the nation's skin over the imperial body," that is to say, to retain Chinese control over non-Chinese territories occupied by the Qing, which included Inner Mongolia and to which the nationalists also hoped to add Outer Mongolia. The resurrection of Chinggis commenced in the 1930s, during the increasing competition for the control of Inner Mongolia among Chinese nationalists, led by Chiang Kai-shek (Jiang Jieshi) and his Nation's Party (the Guomindang, previously abbreviated as KMT), the Chinese Communist Party (CCP), and the Japanese occupation forces and their puppets. In 1935 Chiang Kai-shek was the first to declare Chinggis a Chinese national hero: Chinggis, a Chinese emperor regardless of his ethnicity, was the first Chinese to conquer Russia, and his heirs' long domination over Moscow was taken as a historical precedent for Chiang Kai-shek's ultimate victory over the Chinese communist party, which Chiang saw as an extension of Moscow. In the same year, however, the emerging CCP leader, Mao Zedong, told the Mongols of Inner Mongolia that only by fighting together with the Communists could the Inner Mongolian nation preserve its glorious Chinggisid heritage. In marked contrast to Soviet Communist rhetoric, in which Chinggis was depicted in extremely negative terms, that of the Chinese communist party incorporated Chinggis Khan as a hero and used him as a symbol for its own ends.

In 1939, when the Chinese feared a Japanese occupation of all Inner Mongolia, the Guomindang transferred Chinggis's "relics" from their Ordos shrine eastward, into the province of Gansu. The Communists, however, eventually secured Mongol support, mainly since they promised autonomy to Inner Mongolia, a policy implemented already

Chinggis Khan's mausoleum in Inner Mongolia, China (photograph: Michal Biran)

in 1947 before the Communists' final victory in 1949, which was greatly facilitated by the Mongols' support.[2]

After the Communists' victory, Chinggis's position in the People's Republic of China was modified according to the PRC's ideological shifts and its nationalities policy. It began with a honeymoon in the early 1950s when the state established Chinggis's mausoleum in the Ordos, where his relics (now returned from Gansu) were stored. By erecting the mausoleum the PRC, just like the Qing dynasty beforehand, appropriated the Mongols' cultural capital, and freely manipulated the character of the Chinggis ritual. Thus the Chinese government permitted only one annual ceremony for Chinggis, as opposed to the monthly rituals that

[2] Interestingly, the Japanese also took part in the race for appropriating Chinggis. Japanese tradition identified Chinggis Khan with a tragic Samurai, Minamoto Yoshitsune (1158–1189), whose elder brother Yoritomo ordered him to commit suicide, fearing his popularity. The legend says that Yoshitsune let his vassal die for him, while he escaped northward, managed to get onto the continent and into Mongolia, where he appeared as Temüjin and eventually became Chinggis Khan.

had prevailed before, and this ceremony was fixed to the summer, whereas the main ceremony had previously been held in the spring. The whole ceremony lost much of its religious symbolism and became an entertaining event celebrated with sport matches, dancing, music and propaganda stressing the unity of the nationalities. This Communists' bear hug, which was accompanied by a vast Chinese colonization of Inner Mongolia, was unwelcome for many of the Mongols in China, yet even they had to admit that Chinggis's lot was by then much better in China than in outer Mongolia, where his cult was completely forbidden.

Chinggis was briefly relegated to his classical Soviet position of tyrant-warlord in the late 1950s, but his fortunes were restored when the Sino-Soviet split of the early 1960s turned him into a useful political weapon. Articles in leading Chinese academic journals, while still condemning Chinggis's campaigns in northern China, praised his progressive role as the unifier of the Mongolian tribes, the founder of Mongolian statehood, promoter of East-West relations and the one who started the move toward the reunification of China, and the conquest of Russia. Chinggis's 800th birthday in 1962 was therefore celebrated with great pomp in China – and even in Taiwan – in sharp contrast to its suppression in the People's Republic of Mongolia and despite Soviet protests that "Beijing wiped the blood from Chinggis Khan's hands and gave him a new and progressive role in Chinese history," preferring "a national-bourgeoisie stand" to proletarian internationalism (Hyer 1966: 703).

Chinggis's restoration in China, however, suffered a new setback during the vicissitudes of the Cultural Revolution (1967–1976). There were concerted attacks on the traditional heritage of the Mongols, as on that of the other nationalities in China, including the Chinese themselves. The Mongols were put under pressure to integrate into Han culture and their resistance led to the death of more than twenty thousand Mongols; the Chinggis mausoleum was pillaged, some of its relics destroyed, and the whole site became a salt factory. This violence ended however, with the beginning of reform policy in 1978, under Deng Xiaoping.

The new shift in the minorities policy since the early 1980s brought about the restoration of Chinggis's mausoleum and the renewal of the annual celebrations there under the banner of "Mongols and Han are one family." New Chinese national policy, which emphasizes China as a common homeland of all of its fifty-six nationalities, had a dramatic effect on the re-conceptualization of Chinggis and his heirs. Now the history of each "minority" is considered an integral part of Chinese history, and the historical heritage of the Mongol nationality occupies a pride of place within the larger Chinese heritage. The Mongol conquest is no longer considered as traumatic, or even as foreign rule, but rather as a time during which the Mongolian "minority" ruled over the whole country. Moreover, thanks to its inclusion of Tibetans, Uighurs, and Muslims (all of whom are important parts of China's contemporary mosaic of nationalities) into a "Chinese" state, the Yuan is seen as a key period in the development of China's multi-ethnic identity, a period which contributed decisively to the cohesiveness of the Chinese nation (Qiu 2002: 143). This new interpretation of history has paved the way for a huge increase in Chinggis's popularity in China since the 1990s, a phenomenon paralleled by similar developments in Outer Mongolia and the West. This in turn has resulted in a China-Mongolia competition on appropriating Chinggis.

The Sino-Mongol contest over Chinggis is manifested, for instance, by the race to discover the Khan's tomb. In the year 2000 Chinese archaeologists announced that they had found the tomb of Chinggis on Chinese soil – in the Altai mountains in Xinjiang, an announcement which Mongolia refused to accept – and which has in fact never been proven. In 2003 an American-Japanese expedition working in Mongolia solemnly declared that it had found the tomb in central Mongolia, some 300 km northeast of Ulaanbaatar, a discovery of which Chinese archaeologists remain skeptical. The government of Mongolia, unwilling to disturb the dead, has not so far allowed further excavation of the site, so both identifications remain conjectural. At the same time, the Chinese have tried to make the best of the mausoleum in Inner Mongolia, claiming that it is more important than the secret location of the real tomb. In 2003 the authorities announced their intention to enlarge the existing mausoleum, and to make this out-of-the-way locale into a major tourist attraction which will include a vast "Chinggisland," a huge amusement park. In 2004, as the project encountered financial difficulties, the Chinese government considered turning it into a private Chinese enterprise. This caused huge protests in both Inner and Outer Mongolia, against the attempt "to sell Chinggis to Chinese capitalists," protests which revealed that even Chinese manipulation of Chinggis has its limits.

Nowadays, Chinggis is enjoying the government's favor and is starring as one of China's most prominent national heroes. Chinggis's wax sculpture stands in the National History Museum in Beijing next to the most prominent emperors in Chinese history; he is praised as the first Chinese who conquered Europe, and many books, films and TV series celebrate his achievements, mainly his positive role in unifying the Mongols and enlarging Chinese territories. This successful Chinese appropriation of Chinggis is an impressive testimony to the remarkable ability of Chinese nationalism to transform a national trauma into a national triumph.

RUSSIA

China's successful appropriation of Chinggis Khan is even more striking when compared to the Great Khan's position in Russia, another region conquered by the Mongols which also became the homeland of certain (though less ample) Mongolian groups, notably the Buryat and the Qalmuq. In Russia, Chinggis remains the sum of all fears and a key "Other" against whom Russian nationalism coalesced. This position began with the memory of the bloody Mongol conquest of Russia, which, unlike the situation in the Muslim world and China, remained the only foreign conquest of the country throughout its history. The religious factor also played a significant role: Russia's chronicles depicted Chinggis and the Tatars from an explicitly religious perspective as infidel outsiders motivated by the devil who sought only to harm Orthodox Christians. The conversion to Islam of the Golden Horde, the Chinggisid state which ruled in Russia till 1480, made things even worse, since it meant that the Christian Russians were subject to the inferior and hated Muslims, an especially insulting situation for a people in whose identity the church had such a prominent position. In order to avoid facing the humiliating implications of that situation, Rus' chronicles chose what Halperin termed "an ideology of silence" (Halperin

1985), namely avoiding as much as possible the issues of Tatar conquest, sovereignty, or rule, and reducing Russo-Mongol relations to a series of bloody Tatar "raids." This background facilitated the delegitimization of Mongol rule, known in Russia as the Tatar Yoke, after the fall of the Golden Horde in the early sixteenth century. Russia's disengagement from the Steppe and from Asia was reinforced in the early eighteenth century with its accelerated westernization, introduced by Peter the Great (r. 1672–1725), despite (or because of) Russia's great institutional debt to the Golden Horde (see chapter four). The notion of the "Tatars" as the "Other" was reinforced by confrontations of Imperial Russia with Asian opponents such as the Ottomans, Central Asian Muslims and the Japanese, being employed as late as 1969 during Sino-Soviet military clashes. European notions of superiority and later racist and colonialist ideologies were introduced into Russian historiography. Not only were the Mongols the sum of the Asian stereotypes against which Russia's new identity was built, they were also blamed for the difficulties Russian westernization encountered. Even more than in the heyday of Arab nationalism, in Imperial Russia, especially in the height of Russian nationalism in the nineteenth century, the Tatars were blamed for anything and everything that went wrong with Russian history or contemporary life: isolation from Western Europe, "missing" the Renaissance and Reformation, economic and cultural backwardness, stagnation and even seclusion of women. Russian historical writing in the eighteenth and nineteenth centuries, based on the Rus' chronicles, denied any credit to the years of the Golden Horde rule, refusing even to incorporate the studies of Russian orientalists and archaeologists who dealt – very successfully – with different aspects of the Golden Horde culture. In the twentieth century this national paradigm converged with Marxist views of the Mongols as an undeveloped, reactionary, and feudal nation. The Mongols continued to be portrayed as the greatest disaster in Russian history, and Chinggis Khan, a genius of destruction and an enemy of mankind, was compared to Hitler and, at the height of the Sino-Soviet dispute, also to Mao as a major threat to Russia's safety and world peace.

Post-Soviet Russia did not rush to revise these positions. While some academic works gave a more balanced evaluation of Russia's relations

with the Golden Horde, and acknowledged the Mongols' positive role
in the history of Russia's minorities such as the Tatar and Buryat (see, for
example, Halperin 2004: Gorskii 2000), a recent provocative book,
which claimed, among other things, that the Mongols never conquered
Russia and that the Horde was just another name for Mother Russia,
won much more popularity (Fomenko 1994). Chinggis finds sympathy
among Russia's Mongolian and Turkic minorities, both Muslims –
notably the Tatars (see chapter five) – and Buddhists, mostly among the
Mongolian Buryats and Qalmuqs. Among the contemporary Buryats,
for example, who in the Soviet period were perceived as Chinggis's victims, he is nowadays celebrated both as a part of a previously suppressed
Buddhist culture and as a powerful political symbol, both of the Buryat
nationality and of a pan-Mongol unity (Skrunnikova 2005). More
surprisingly, Chinggis is also popular in the circles of the extreme right
and among Russia's post-Soviet communists, both connected to the
Eurasian movement. Eurasianism, the counter-current of the dominant
Russian discourse, claims that Russia was neither European nor Asian
but a world unto itself. This view, best represented by Trubetzkoi's 1925
article "The Legacy of Genghis Khan: A Perspective on Russian History
not from the West but from the East," (Trubetskoi 1991) argued that
Chinggis Khan was the father of Russia: the Mongol conquest was a central event of Russian history; its impact on Russia was not entirely
negative; Russian expansion eastward was one of the most important
aspects of Russian history; and Russia's unique position as connecting
East and West should become a major factor in determining its future
policy. The Eurasianists enjoyed a certain popularity among Russian
émigrés in the 1920s but remained marginal to the general historical
discourse in Russia. Today, contemporary Eurasianists in Russia's
extreme right are still presenting themselves as Chinggis's "spiritual
children." They see Russia as a legitimate successor to Chinggis's
empire that should continue his mission of uniting the Eurasian geopolitical space through further expansion under an autocratic leadership (see website *http://arcto.ru/modules.php?name = News&file =
article&sid = 1182*; Khazanov 2003). Despite these exceptions, on the
whole Russia has not appropriated Chinggis, but rather kept him in the
villain's role.

THE WEST

Chinggis never conquered Western Europe, yet his unique career awarded him a certain place in Western collective memory. Chinggis was an outsider, an oriental ruler, whose figure shifted between conflicting images, first due to the actual Mongol threat on Europe and later due to fluctuating images of the East, especially of China (to which he was connected from Marco Polo onward) and of the Ottomans (who were widely considered to be offspring of the Mongols). In religious terms, Chinggis changed from the Scourge of God and the Antichrist in the first half of the thirteenth century into a true believer in God in the fourteenth-century *Travels of John of Mandeville* and then to an example of the rule of reason and talent that ignores religion in the early Enlightenment. Politically, Chinggis shifted from being an ideal, wise, and sometimes even romantic ruler, in Polo's and Chaucer's works of the fourteenth century, to the oriental despot *par excellance* in the late Enlightenment. His positive image was at its height in the fourteenth century, with the growing European contacts with Asia, after the Mongols ceased to be a threat to Europe and before the Ottomans became one, and in the late seventeenth to early eighteenth century as part of the Europeans' enthusiasm for China and their coming to terms with the Ottomans, as well as with European awareness of the continuous Chinggisid legacy in many parts of Asia. The early eighteenth century also saw the publication of the first biography of Chinggis in Europe, Petis de la Croix's (1622–1695) *Histoire du Grand Genghizcan* (The History of Genghizcan the Great), published after his death, in 1710, and translated into English in 1722. The author, a "secretary and interpreter to the King [of France] in the Turkish and Arabic languages," wrote his book in response to a French minister's request. The latter became interested in Chinggis as a model of rulership after hearing de la Croix's translation of an Ottoman poem about the Great Khan. In general, the Ottomans were the main channel through which western historical study of Chinggis began, and Muslim sources were the main building blocks for retrieving the Khan's biography. In de la Croix's case this resulted in a rather balanced and highly influential historical narrative.

The early eighteenth century also saw the Jesuit translation of a Chinese biography of Chinggis based on a Qing compilation, and in addition he became the hero of two successful European plays: Voltaire's *Orphelin de la Chine* (The Orphan of China, 1755) and Daw's *Zingis* (1768), the enthusiastic advertisement for which is cited at the head of this chapter. This picture, however, changed drastically from the late eighteenth century, with the later Enlightenment's disillusionment with China and the East and the growth of the notion of western superiority. Montesquieu (1685–1755) and Adam Smith (1723–1790) portrayed Chinggis as a savage, barbarian tyrant and he soon became a model for oriental despotism. In the nineteenth century this was augmented with racial concepts, in which the Mongols gave their name to the yellow race, identified with servility, stagnation and primitivism; and Down's syndrome (Trisomy 21), a genetic defect associated with low intelligence and even degeneration, came to be known as Mongolism. Indeed the major work devoted to the Mongols in the early nineteenth century, D'Ohsson's four volume *Histoire des mongols depuis Tchinguiz Khan jusqu'a Timour Bey ou Tamerlane* (History of the Mongols from Chinggis Khan to Temür Bey or Tamerlane) depicted Chinggis and the Mongols in a rather grim light. D'Ohsson, an Armenian diplomat in the service of the Swedish embassy in Istanbul and later in Paris, who worked mainly with Muslim sources (including many Mamluk Arabic works), commemorated Chinggis as the one who said: "The greatest joy a man can know is to conquer his enemies and drive them before him, to ride their horses and take away their possessions, to see the faces of those who were dear to them bedewed with tears, and to clasp their wives and daughters in his arms"(D'Ohsson 1834–1835: 1: 404, based on Rashid al-Din). The despotic and cruel rule of the Mongols, he noted, made an extraordinarily ugly picture, but it was needed for an understanding of the events of the thirteenth and fourteenth centuries (D'Ohsson 1834–1835: 1: V–VII).

Even though he had never completely lost his charm as the noble savage and the genius warrior, Chinggis continued to be depicted as a cruel barbarian despot, associated first and foremost with death and destruction, from the nineteenth century onward. It was this image of him which passed to the Middle East, to be adopted by Arab and Iranian nationalists, as discussed in chapter five.

Chinggis's image has, however, undergone a dramatic change in the last part of the twentieth century and in the first years of the twenty-first century. Globalization, the new universal supranational ideology, enabled the West to appropriate Chinggis as an insider, not an outsider, the father of the first globalization. Chinggis became one of the makers of the modern world, including the West, and therefore a much more complex and popular figure than before. The reemergence of the East as a significant power in world history, a renewed fascination with the exotic "other," and the major advance of academic study of the Mongols in recent decades also contributed to his growing popularity. In 1995 the Washington Post, perhaps jokingly, elected Chinggis as "the man of the (second) millennium," noting that he "has combined humanistic civilization and barbarism in one body perfectly" (see website *http://www.sconet.state.oh.us/Communications_office/Speeches/1999/osb a.asp*), and Chinggis loomed large in millennial conclusions of other forums too. This does not mean that Chinggis has lost his association with death and destruction – when the American president was called Genghis Bush on the eve of his invasion to Iraq it certainly was not a compliment – but this is no longer his only or major characteristic. The Oxford scientists' claim of 2003, that they had discovered a specific DNA of the Y chromosome common to some 16 million males in the Old World who are thought to be Chinggis's descendants, a discovery which led western reporters to crown Chinggis as the most prolific lover the world had ever encountered, also considerably added to his charm (Zerjal et al. 2003: 717–721).

Also influential were a series of art exhibitions, notably the Metropolitan Museum of New York's 2003 exhibition "The Legacy of Genghis Khan: Courtly Art and Culture in Western Asia, 1256–1353" and Bonn's 2005 "Dschingis Khan und seine Erben," which portrayed the artistic dialogue under the Mongols, and a number of books and TV films which celebrated Chinggis's achievements, stressing – like the present study – that his legacy has been far more complex and constructive than that of havoc and massacre on a large scale.

Eight hundred years after the 1206 *quriltai*, Chinggis Khan is very much alive in the world's collective memory, despite the fact that the nomadic world in which he rose to power and in whose terms he should be understood has almost vanished completely. Moreover, the plasticity that his figure acquired throughout these eight hundred years is impressive: Chinggis is known as one of the great enemies of culture, as a cultural ancestor, and as a great promoter of cross-cultural contacts. Religiously, Chinggis is conceived as an important Buddhist deity; the locus of shamanic cults; the Antichrist; a friend of God; a Muslim *hanif* (early monotheist); and an arch-enemy of Islam. Chinggis is also invoked as a genius conqueror and strategist; a savage barbarian and a sophisticated law giver. Politically, he shifts from the oriental despot *par excellence* up to the harbinger of democracy, celebrated in between as the unifier of Mongolia; the harbinger of Chinese unification and of Eurasian unity; the revered forefather of Chinese and Muslim dynasties and the arch enemy against which other states and empires coalesced their identity. Chinggis was a Mongol; nowadays he is also Chinese, Kazakh, Buryat and "man of the world" – the father of the first globalization.

This multiple image and its continuous evolution is partially explained by the phenomenal scope of Chinggis's career which made him remembered in each of the realms on which he had an impact – Mongolia, China, the Muslim world, Russia, and Western Europe. Another reason is the range of activities on which Chinggis left an enduring mark: military exploits; establishing an enduring and functioning empire; promulgation of law; and causing massive destruction, which eventually, however, also laid the foundation for future intensive cross-cultural contacts. Moreover, Chinggis did not remain only an historical figure: his life has inspired a host of epic myths, legends, and literary works from Buddhist compilations to English and French plays, Hollywood movies, Chinese TV series, Muslim chronicles, eposes and religious works, and historical novels from around the world. These helped to keep him in the social memory and magnified his symbolic power as an individual who is seen as transcending all others and therefore can become a focus of social and political collectiveness.

While in the West the use of the Chinggis symbol has been merely an intellectual pursuit, in Mongolia, China, and even Russia, and certainly in the Muslim world, the Great Khan has played an important role in the construction of political identities and entities, at least in certain periods. Chinggis has been invoked not only for justifying conquests but mainly for legitimizing political power in its different forms. His diverse role in the various parts of the world has been determined mostly due to his changing value for constructing collective political identities – universal, dynastic, tribal, and national. The unprecedented scope of his achievements has made him an extremely useful model for governments with universal aspirations, such as Tamerlane's empire, Yuan and Qing China, and even Mamluk Egypt and Imperial Russia, in both the Mongols served as the key "other" against whom the empires asserted their identity. The Chinggisid principle, another by-product of Chinggis's unique success, secured his position as a revered progenitor of dynasties and tribes wherever his descendants retained power and as long as history remained perceived in dynastic or genealogical terms, i.e., into the nineteenth century in certain parts of the world, notably Central Asia. The rise of nationalism as the world's major political ideology therefore had an enormous impact on Chinggis's appropriation. Theoretically, nationalism limited Chinggis's relevance only to places where there were Mongols, and indeed it turned him into a *persona non grata* in most of the Muslim world. Yet it also made him a national hero not only of Mongolia, but also of the whole of China and, more hesitantly, also of other Mongolian people, such as the Buryats, the Qalmuqs, and even among the Turkic and Muslim Tatars and Kazakhs. The rise of modern universal, supra-national, political concepts, mainly Communism and globalization, also in turn influenced Chinggis's image and his position as a national symbol, either for worse, in the case of Communism, or for better, in globalization's case. The changing political circumstances continue to shape and reshape Chinggis's image in different parts of the world.

Due to his marginalization in the modern Muslim world, and because he was not a Muslim, Chinggis is not automatically associated with the Muslim world. Yet, as this book has attempted to demonstrate, Chinggis and his heirs have been closely connected with the world of Islam and have played a significant role in its pre-modern configuration. Muslims were among Temüjin's first supporters, even prior to his enthronement as Chinggis Khan, and they played a certain role in the success of his conquests. More significant, it was Chinggis's campaign into the Muslim world which completed his transformation from a successful nomadic chieftain on the fringes of China to world conqueror of an unparalleled scale. The speedy annihilation of the Khwarazm Shah's power not only drastically enlarged the territories and manpower under Chinggis's control, but also enhanced his prestige and bolstered his public image as someone pre-destined by Heaven to conquer the entire world. Moreover, this invasion also closely exposed him to a sedentary culture different from that of China, the major reference point of Mongolian nomads throughout history. The stock of administrative, military and cultural tools under Chinggis's disposal, when he turned to organize his newly acquired empire, was therefore much more diverse than that which had been available to former nomadic conquerors. The creative use Chinggis and his heirs found for the diverse traditions of their subjects was soon to become one of the main hallmarks of their multi-cultural empire. Muslim cultural heritage was highly appreciated by the Mongols, not least due to the nomadic background of the Muslim Turks, and it became an important component of the Mongol imperial enterprise.

This should not make us forget that the Muslims also suffered immensely from Chinggis's campaigns and from those of his heirs, the infamous destruction of Baghdad being the most renowned example. Yet after recovering from the initial shock of the Mongol invasions, many Muslims were quick to exploit the new opportunities offered by the Chinggisid age, in terms of trade, employment, travel, cultural and scientific exchange, and conversion. The Mongol period was a key period in the expansion of Islam not least because in three out of four of the Mongol khanates Islam managed to conqueror its conquerors: namely, the Mongols embraced Islam.

The Islamization of the Mongols opened a new stage in the relations between Chinggis Khan and the world of Islam. Chinggis's political legacy – notably the Chinggisid principle and the Yasa – were adopted by his Muslim heirs and even by some non-Chinggisid rulers and dynasties, and new Muslim people coalesced around different Chinggisid branches or around names of Chinggisid princes. The history of

Chinggis and his heirs became an integral part of Muslim historiography and of other literary genres, and Chinggis's position as the revered forefather of many Muslim dynasties and peoples won him a place of prominence in Muslim literary tradition, unchallenged in the post-Muhammadan world by any other non-Muslim.

The rise of nationalism, as discussed above, drove Chinggis into the fringes of the Muslim collective memory and returned him to his initial role of the ultimate villain. But this modern vilification and marginality should not disguise the debt the Muslim world owes to the nomadic conqueror who tumbled into it in the early thirteenth century: the legacy of the Mongols in the Muslim world includes, aside from huge amounts of death and desolation, a long-lasting cultural effervescence, thriving artistic and scientific exchange, and booming international trade, as well as new and enduring forms of legitimacy and law, considerable expansion of the world of Islam, and the emergence of new Muslim peoples. In terms of political culture, ethnic composition, and intellectual and artistic traditions, it is impossible to understand the post-thirteenth century Muslim world without taking into account the Chinggisid legacy.

SELECTED BIBLIOGRAPHY

GENERAL

The bibliography includes the main secondary sources consulted for the different chapters (with preference to works in English, which are more accessible), as well as full references to works mentioned in the notes. Here I would like to refer to some general works as well as to mention some of the primary sources about Chinggis, which are available in English translation.

The best introduction to the Mongol empire is still David O. Morgan's *The Mongols* (Oxford, 1986; an updated edition is anticipated soon). For a quick glance on what's new in the field of Mongol studies at least up to 1999, see Peter Jackson (2000), "The State of Research: The Mongol Empire, 1986–1999" *Journal of Medieval History*, 26: 189–210. The works of Thomas T. Allsen, the most prominent historian of the Mongol empire active today, deserves a special mention – and are well attested in the bibliography below – since they, most notably his *Culture and Conquest in Mongol Eurasia* (Cambridge, 2001), contributed immensely to a more complete understanding of the Chinggisid enterprise. Two recent collected volumes, which contain many useful articles on the Mongols, are also worth mentioning. These are *The Mongol Empire and its Legacy* (Leiden, 1999), edited by Reuven Amitai-Preiss and David O. Morgan, and *Mongols, Turks and Others: Eurasian Nomads and the Outside World* (Leiden, 2005), edited by Reuven Amitai and Michal Biran. From the many biographies of Chinggis, the most scholarly is Paul Ratchnevsky's, *Genghis Khan: His Life and Times* (trans. Thomas Haining, Oxford, 1991), the English translation of which is even better than the 1983 German original. Among more recent Chinggis's books, Jack Weatherford's *Genghis Khan and the Making of the Modern World* (New

York, 2003; rpt. 2004), the only biography of Chinggis that hit the New York Times bestsellers' list, is the most enjoyable. Though the historical details are not always accurate, Weatherford, an anthropologist who spent much time in Mongolia, certainly succeeded in giving the feeling of what life was like there by the thirteenth century.

Many sources for Chinggis's life are now available in English translation. First among them is the *Secret History*, the only Mongol source narrating Chinggis's life. The magisterial translation of Igor de Rachewiltz, published in 2004, whose notes were widely used in this book, is by far the best academic edition (DeRachewiltz, Igor, trans. 2004, *The Secret History of the Mongols*. Leiden, 2 vols). For the general reader, however, Paul Kahn's adaptation of the text (Kahn, Paul 1998: *The Secret History of the Mongols:the Origins of Chinggis Khan*. Boston) is no less useful and much less frightening. The works of the great Persian historians, Juwayni and Rashid al-Din are now fully available in English (Juvaini, ʿAta Malik 1997. *Genghis Khan: History of World Conqueror*. Trans. J. A. Boyle. Reprint of the 2 volumes edition of Manchester, 1958; Rashid al-Din, 1998–1999. *Jami'u't-tawarikh (sic) Compendium of Chronicles*. Trans. W.M. Thackston. Cambridge, Mass, 3 vols.), and there is also an old and not very faithful translation of Juzjani's Persian chronicle written in India (Juzjani, Minhaj al-Din, 1881. *Tabaqat-i Nasiri*. Trans. H.G. Raverty. London, 2 vols). There is also a full English translation of the travels of Ibn Battuta which include details about Chinggis and his heirs (Gibb, H.A. R, trans. 1956–1994. *The Travels of Ibn Battuta*. London, 4 vols).

Chinese sources on Chinggis are usually less accessible, though one should mention Walley's translation of the memoirs of the Daoist Patriarch, Chang Chun, who had met Chinggis in Central Asia (Li Zhichang [Li Chih-chang], 1931. *Travels of an Alchemist*. Trans. A. Waley. London). European sources on the Mongols, though originating in the post-Chinggisid era, also include information on the Great Khan. See, for example, the travelogues of the friars John of Plano Carpini (in Dawson, Christopher, trans, 1955. *The Mongol Mission*. New York [Rpt. As *Mission to Asia*]) and William of Rubruck (in Jackson, Peter, trans. and ed., with assistance of D. Morgan, 1990. *The Mission of Friar William of Rubruck*. London), as well as the many editions of Marco Polo's travels (e.g., Marco Polo, 1992. *The Travels*. Ed. and trans. H. Yule and H. Cordier. Reprinted, NewYork, 2 vols). A selection of translated paragraphs on the Mongols and a very useful annotated bibliography of translated sources on the Mongols in general appear in George Lane's *Genghis Khan and Mongol Rule* (Westport, CT, 2004).

CHAPTER 1

Allsen, Thomas T. 1996. "Spiritual Geography and Political Legitimacy in the Eastern Steppe," in *Ideology and the Early State*, eds. H. Claessen and J. Oosten. 116–135. Leiden.

Barfield, Thomas J. 1989. *The Perilious Frontier: Nomadic Empires and China*. Oxford.

Barthold, V. V. 1968. *Turkestan down to the Mongol Invasion*. trans. V. Minorsky, London. Fourth edition.

Bentley, Jerry, 1993. *Old World Encounters*. NewYork.

Biran, Michal 2005. *The Qara Khitai Empire in Eurasian History: Between China and the Islamic World*. Cambridge.

Buell, Paul D. 1992. "Early Mongol Expansion in Western Siberia and Turkestan (1207–1219) – A Reconstruction," *Central Asiatic Journal* 36: 1–32.

Christian, David 1998. *A History of Russia, Central Asia and Mongolia Vol. 1*. Oxford.

Di Cosmo Nicola, 1999. "State Formation and Periodization in Inner Asian History," *Journal of World History*, 10: 1–40.

Di Cosmo, Nicola 2002. "Introduction: Inner Asian Ways of Warfare," in *Warfare in Inner Asian History (500–1800)*, ed. N. Di Cosmo. Leiden.

Golden, Peter. B. 1982. "Imperial Ideology and the Sources of Political Unity amongst the Pre-Chinggisid Nomads of Western Eurasia," *Archivum Eurasiae Medii Aevi*, 2: 37–77.

Ibn Khaldun, ʿAbd al-Rahman 1957. *Kitab al-ʿibar*. Beirut. 7 vols.

Khazanov, Anatoly M. 1984. *Nomads and the Outside World*. Cambridge.

Morgan, David O. 1988. *Medieval Persia, 1040–1797*. London.

Wittfogel, Karl. and Feng Chia-sheng 1949. *History of Chinese Society: Liao 907–1125*. Philadelphia: American Philosophical Society.

Sinor, Denis, ed. 1994. *The Cambridge History of Early Inner Asia*. Cambridge.

Twitchett, Denis and Herbert Franke, eds. 1994. *The Cambridge History of China, Vol. 6: Alien Regimes and Border States 907–1368*. Cambridge.

CHAPTERS 2 AND 3

Aigle, Denis 2004. "Le grand yasa de Gengis Khan, l'empire, la culture mongole et la charia," *Journal of the Economic and Social History of the Orient* 47: 31–79.

Allsen, Thomas T. 1994. "The Rise of the Mongol Empire and Mongolian Rule in North China," in *The Cambridge History of China vol. 6:Alien states and Border Regimes 907–1368*, eds. D. Twitchett and H. Franke. 329–333. Cambridge.

Allsen, Thomas T. 2004. "Technologies of Governance in the Mongolian Empire: A Geographical Survey," paper given in the MIASU Symposium on Inner Asian Statecrafts and Technologies of Governance, Cambridge UK, March 18–19, 2004.

Amitai, Reuven and Michal Biran, eds. 2005. *Mongols, Turks and Others: Eurasian Nomads and the Outside World.* Leiden.

Amitai-Preiss, Reuven 1998. "Mongol Imperial Ideology and the Ilkhanid War against the Mamluks," in R. Amitai-Preiss and D. O. Morgan 59–72.

Jackson, Peter 2005a. "The Mongols and the Faith of the Conquered," in Amitai and Biran, 245–290.

Kennedy, E. S. 1991. "An Astrological History Based on the Career of Genghis Khan," in *Quest for Understanding:Arabic and Islamic Studies in Memory of Malcolm H. Kerr*, ed. S. Seikali, R. Ballbaki and P. Dodd. 223–231. Beirut.

Lattimore, Owen 1963. "The Geography of Chingis Khan," *Geographical Journal*, 129:1–7.

Morgan, David O. 2005. "The Yasa of Chinggis Khan Revisited," in Amitai and Biran, 291–308.

May, Timothy 2004. "The Mechanics of Conquest and Governance:The Rise and Expansion of the Mongol Empire 1185–1265," Ph.d Dissertation, University of Wisconsin-Madison.

De Rachewiltz, Igor 1989. "The Title Chinggis Khan/Qaghan Reexamined," in *Gedanke und Wirkung. Feschchrift zum 90 Geburstag von Nikolaus Poppe*, ed. W. Heissig and K. Sagaster. 281–298. Wiesbaden.

De Rachewiltz, Igor 1993. "Some Reflexions on Chinggis Khan's *Jasaj*," *East Asian History*, 6: 91–104.

Ratchnevsky, Paul 1991. *Genghis Khan: His Life and Times* Tr. Thomas Haining. Oxford.

Smith, John M. 1993–4. "Demographic Considerations in Mongol Siege Warfare," *Archivum Ottomanicum*, 13: 329–334.

Spuler, B. 1972. *History of the Mongols: Based on Eastern and Western Accounts of the 13th and 14th Centuries*. London.

Togan, Isenbike 1998. *Flexibility and Limitation in Steppe Formations: The Kerait Khanate and Chinggis Khan*. Leiden.

Weatherford, Jack 2004. *Genghis Khan and the Making of the Modern World*. New York.

CHAPTER 4

Abu-Lughod, Janet 1989. *Before European Hegemony*. Oxford and New York.

Allsen, Thomas T. 1997a. *Commodity and Exchange in the Mongol Empire: A Cultural History of Islamic Textiles*. Cambridge.

Allsen, Thomas T. 2001. *Culture and Conquest of Mongol Eurasia*. Cambridge.

Allsen, Thomas T. 1997b. "Ever Closer Encounters: The Appropriation of Culture and the Apportionment of Peoples in the Mongol Empire," *Journal of Early Modern History*, 1: 2–23.

Allsen, Thomas T. 1989a. *Mongol Imperialism: The Policies of the Great Qan Möngke in China, Russia and the Islamic Lands*. Berkeley.

Allsen, Thomas T. 1989b "Mongolian Princes and their Merchant Partners 1200–1260," *Asia Major*, 2: 83–126.

Allsen, Thomas T. 2000. "The Rasulid Hexaglot in its Eurasian Cultural Context," in *The King's Dictionary*. Ed. and tr. P.B. Golden. 25–49. Leiden.

Amitai-Preiss, Reuven 1995. Mongols and Mamluks: The Mamluk-Ilkhanid War, 1260–1281. Cambridge.

Amitai-Preiss, Reuven and David O. Morgan, eds. 1999. *The Mongol Empire and its Legacy*. Leiden.

Biran, Michal 1997. *Qaidu and the Rise of the Independent Mongol State in Central Asia*. Richmond, Surrey.

Biran, Michal 2004. "The Mongol Transformation: From the Steppe to Eurasian Empire," *Medieval Encounters*, 10: 338–361.

Boyle, John .A., ed. 1968. *The Cambridge History of Iran Vol. 5: The Saljuq and Mongol Periods*. Cambridge.

Comaroff, Linda and S. Carboni, eds. 2003. *The Legacy of Genghis Khan: Courtly Art and Culture in Western Asia, 1256–1353*. New York and New Haven.

Fleischer, Cornell H. 1986. *Bureaucrat and Intellectual in the Ottoman Empire: The Historian Mustafa Ali (1541–1600)*. Princeton.

Fletcher, Joseph 1986. "The Mongols: Ecological and Social perspectives," *Harvard Journal of Asiatic Studies*, 46: 1–46.

Foltz, Richard C. 1998. *Mughal India and Central Asia*. Oxford-Karachi.

Frank, Andre G. 1998. *ReOrient: Global Economy in the Asian Age.* Berkeley.

Fregner, Bert 1997. "Iran under Ilkhanid Rule in a World History Perspective," in *L'Iran face a la domination mongole*, ed. D. Aigle. Tehran.

Golden, Peter B. 1992. *An Introduction to the History of the Turkic People.* Wiesbaden.

Golden, Peter B. 2000. " 'I will give the people unto thee,': The Chinggisid Conquests and their Aftermath in the Turkic World," *Journal of the Royal Asiatic Society* Series 3, 10: 21–41.

Haidar, Mansura 1992. "The Yasai Chingizi (Tura) in the Medieval Indian Sources," in *Mongolia: Culture, Economy, Politics*, ed. R.C. Sharma *et.al.* 53–65. New Delhi.

Halperin, Charles J. 1983. "Russia in the Mongol Empire in Comparative Perspective," *Harvard Journal of Asiatic Studies*, 43: 239–261.

Heywood, Colin 2000. "Filling the Black Hole: the emergence of the Bithynian Atamanates," in *The Great Ottoman-Turkish Civilisation*, ed. K. Çiçek *et al* 1: 107–115. Ankara.

Jackson, Peter 1978. "The Dissolution of the Mongol Empire," *Central Asiatic Journal* 22:186–244.

Jackson, Peter 1999. *The Delhi Sultanate: A Political and Military History.* Cambridge.

Lane, George 2003. *Early Mongol Rule in Thirteenth Century Iran: A Persian Renaissance.* Richmond, Surrey.

Leslie, Donald D. 1988. *Islam in Traditional China*. Canberra.

Lewis, Archibald 1988. *Nomads and Crusades 1000–1368*. Bloomington.

Lewis, Bernard 1993. "The Mongols, the Turks and Muslim Polity," in his *Islam in History: Ideas, People and Events in the Middle East*. 2nd ed. Chicago. (The article was originally published in 1968).

Lindner, R.P. 1998. "How Mongol Were the Early Ottomans?" in Amitai-Preiss and Morgan, 282–289.

Manz, Beatrice F. 1989. *The Rise and Rule of Tamerlane.* Cambridge.

Manz, Beatrice F. 1994. "Historical Introduction," in *Central Asia in Historical Perspective*, Ed. B.F. Manz. Boulder: Westview Press.

Manz, Beatrice F. 2000. "Mongol History Rewritten and Relived," *Revue des mondes musulmans et de la méditerranée*, 89–90: 129–149.

Manz, Beatrice F. 2002. "Tamerlane's Career and its Uses," *Journal of World History*, 13:1–25.

McChesney, Robert D. 1996. *Central Asia: Foundations of Change*. Princeton.

McChesney, Robert D. 2000. "Zamzam Water on a White Felt Carpet: Adapting Mongol Ways in Muslim Central Asia, 1550–1650," in *Religion, Customary Law and Nomadic Technology*, ed. M. Gervers and W. Schlepp. 63–80. Toronto.

McNeill, William H. 1977. *Plagues and People*. New York.

De Rachewiltz, Igor, et.al., eds. 1993. *In The Service of the Khan: Eminent Personalities of the Early Mongol –Yuan Period*. Wiesbaden.

Wink, Andre 1997. *Al-Hind:The Making of the Indo-Islamic World.Vol. 2:The Slave Kings and the Islamic Conquest 11th–13th Centuries*. Leiden.

CHAPTER 5

Abu al-Ghazi Bahadur Khan 1970. *Histoire des Mongols et des Tatars*. Trans. P. I. Desmaisons. Rpt. Amsterdam and St. Leonards.

Aigle, Denise 2000. "Les transformations d'un mythe d'origine: L'example de Gengis Khan et de Tamerlan," *Revue des mondes musulmans et de la méditerranée*, 89–90: 151–168.

Amitai, Reuven 2004. "Did Chinggis Khan has a Jewish Teacher?" *Journal of the American Oriental Society* 124 (4): 691–705.

Bregel, Yuri 1982. "Tribal Tradition and Ethnic History: The Early Rulers of the Qongrat according to Munis," *Asian and African Studies* 16: 357–398.

Bregel, Yuri, trans. 1997. *Fidaws al-Iqbal: History of Khwarazm*, by Shir Muhammad Mirab Munis and Muhammad Mirza Mirab Agahi. Leiden.

Bulag, Uradyn E. 1994 "Dark Quadrangle in Central Asia: Empires, Ethnogenesis, Scholars and Nation-States," *Central Asian Studies*, 13 (4): 459–478.

Choueiri, Youssef M. 2000. *Arab Nationalism – A History: Nation and State in the Arab World*. Oxford.

Darwazah, Muhammad 'Izzat 1929. *Durus al-ta'rikh al-'arabi min aqdam al-azmina hatta al-an*. (Lessons of Arab History: From Antiquity to the Present Time). Cairo.

Daniyarov, Kalibak 1998. *Al'ternativnay a istoriya Kazakhstana*. (Alternative History of Kazakhstan). Almaty.

Daniiarov, Kalibak 2001. *Istoriia Tsingis Khana* (History of Chinggis Khan). Almaty.

De Rachewiltz, Igor 1994. "The Mongols Rethink their Early History," in *The East and the Meaning of History: (International Conference 23–27 November 1992).* 357–380. Rome.

DeWeese, Devin 1993. *Islamization and Native Religion in the Golden Horde.* University Park, PA.

Dobrovits, Mihali 1994. "The Turco-Mongolian Tradition of Common Origin and the Historiography in Fifteenth Century Central Asia," *Acta Orientalia (Hungaria),* 47 / 3: 269–277.

Frank, Allen J. 1998. *Islamic Historiography and the Bulghar Identity among the Tatars and Bashkirs of Russia.* Leiden.

Haarmann, Ulrich 2001. "Mongols and Mamluks. Forgotten Villains and Heroes of Arab History," in *Crisis and Memory in Islamic Societies.* Proceedings of the Third Summer Academy of the Working Group Modernity and Islam Held at the Orient Institute of the German Oriental Society in Beirut , ed. A. Neuwirth and A. Pflitsch (Beiruter Texte und Studien, 77). 165–176. Beirut.

al-Huwayri, Mahmud 1996. *Misr fi al-ʿusur al-wusta* (Medieval Egypt). al-Haram.

Islam Niya, Faridun 2004. *Nigahi bih taʾrikh-i Iran baʾd al-islam* (Aspects of Iranian Islamic History). Urumiyya.

Ivanics, Mária and Mirkasym A. Usmanov, 2002. *Das Buch der Dschingis-Legende. (Däftär-i Dschingis-namä).* Studia Uralo-Altaica 44. Szeged.

Ivanics, Mária, forthcoming. *Das Buch der Dschingis-Legende.* (German translation).

Kannedy, Hugh 1998. *The Historiography of Islamic Egypt.* Cambridge.

Lewisohn, L. 1995. *Beyond Faith and Infidelity: The Sufi Poetry and Teaching of Mahmud Shabistari.* Richmond, Surrey.

Mackey, Sandra 1996. *The Iranians: Persia, Islam and the Soul of a Nation.* New York and London.

Makarius, Shahin 2003. *Taʾrikh Iran* (History of Iran). Cairo.

Munajjim Bashi, Ahmad b. Lutfallah 1868. *Sakhayif al-akhbar.* Istanbul, 3 vols.

Nawdhari, ʾIzzatallah 2004. *Iran wa-taʾrikh* (Iran and History). Shiraz.

al-Nuwayri, Shihab al-Din Ahmad b. ʿAbd al-Wahhab 1984. *Nihayat al-arab fi funun al-adab.* Vol. 27, ed. F. ʿAshur. Cairo.

Penahi, Muhammad Ahmad 2002. *Chingiz-i Moghul* (Chinggis the Mongol). Tehran.

Pope, Nicole and Pope, Hugh 1997. *Turkey Unveiled: Atatürk and After*. London: John Murray.

al-Qawsi, Yusuf Ahmad and Abbas Mahmud al-Sharif 1966. *al-Ta'rikh al-'arabi al-islami* (Arabic Islamic History). Cairo.

Quinn, Sheila 2000. *HistoricalWriting during the Reign of Shah 'Abbas: Ideology, Imitation and Legitimacy in Safawid Chronicles*. Salt Lake City.

al-Rafi'i, 'Abd al-Rahman and Sa'id 'Ashur 1970. *Misr fi al-'usur al-wusta* (Medieval Egypt). Cairo.

Razi, Najm al-Din Daya 1982. *The Path of God's Bondsmen from Origin to Return* (Mersad al-'ebad men mabda' ela 'l-ma'ad). Trans. H. Algar. Delmar, NY.

Sa'id, Amin 1959. *al-Jumhuriyya al-'arabiyya al-muttahida* (The United Arab Republic). Cairo.

Al-Sarjani, Raghib 2006. *Kissat al-Tatar min al-bidaya ila 'Ayn Jalut*. Cairo.

Shabankarah'i, Muhammad b. ʿAli 1984, *Majmaʿ al-ansab*. Ed. M. H. Muhhadith. Tehran.

Shihabi, Mustafa Ahmad and Ibrahim Samir Sayf al-Din 1965. *al-Ta'rikh al-musawwar* (An Illustrated History). Cairo.

al-Subki, Taj al-Din Abi Nasr 1964. *Tabaqat al-shafi'iyya al-kubra*. Allepo. 10 volumes.

Tamer, Zakaria 1985. *Tigers on the Tenth Day and Other Stories*. Trans. D. Johnson-Davies. London, Melbourne, NewYork.

Türk Ansiklopedisi 1964; q.v. Çingiz Han; ÇingizYasasi.

Woods, John 1990. "Timur's Genealogy," in *Intellectual Studies on Islam: Essays Written in Honor of Martin B. Dickson*. Ed. M. M. Mazzaoui and V. B. Moreen. 82–125. Salt Lake City.

Zaydan, Jurji 1902–5. *Ta'rikh al-tamaddun al-islami* (History of Islamic Civilization). Cairo. 5 volumes.

Zinukhov, Aleksandr 2005. *Tsingiskhan – syn Isaaka kievskovo* (Chinggis Khan- Son of Isaac of Kiev). Kharkov.

CHAPTER 6

Atwood, Christopher P. 2004. *Encyclopedia of Mongolia and the Mongol Empire*. NewYork.

Bawden, Charles. R. 1968. *The Modern History of Mongolia*. London.

Crossley, Pamela. K. 1999. *A Translucent Mirror: History and Identity in Qing Imperial Ideology*. Berkeley.

D'Ohsson, C.M. 1834–5. *Histoire des Mongols depuis Tchinguis Khan jusqu'a Timour Bey.* The Hague. 4 vols.

Dow, Alexander 1768. *Zingis: A Tragedy.* London.

Elverskog, John 1999. "Superscribing the Hegemonic Image of Chinggis Khan in the *Erdeni Tunumal Sudur*," in *Return to the Silk Routes: Current Scandinavian Research on Central Asia*, ed. M. Juntunen and B. N. Schlyter. 75–86. New York and London.

Elverskog, John 2003. *The Jewel Translucent Sutra.* Leiden.

Enkhtuvshin, B. and J. Tsolmon, eds. 2003. *Chinggis Khan and Contemporary Era.* Ulaanbaatar.

Farquhar, David M. 1968. "The Origins of the Manchu's Mongolian Policy," in *The Chinese World Order*, ed. J. K. Fairbank. 198–205. Cambridge, MA.

Gorskii, A. A. 2000. *Moskva i Orda* (Moscow and the Horde). Moscow.

Halperin, Charles J. 1985. *Russia and the Golden Horde.* Bloomington.

Halperin, Charles J. 2004. "Omissions of National Memory: Russian Historiography on the Golden Horde as Politics of Inclusion and Exclusion," *Ab Imperio* 4/3.

Hangin, John G 1973. *Köke Sudur (the Blue Chronicle) A Study of the First Mongolian Historical Novel by Injannasi.* Wiesbaden.

Heissig, Walther 1980. *The Religions of Mongolia.* Berkeley.

Hyer, Paul 1966. "The Reevaluation of Chinggis Khan: Its Role in the Sino-Soviet Dispute," *Asian Survey*: 696–705.

Jackson, Peter 2005b. *The Mongols and the West.* Harlow.

Jagchid, Sechin 1988. *Essays in Mongolian Studies.* Provo.

Kaplonski, Ch. 2004. *Truth, History and Politics in Monglia: The Memory of Heroes.* London and New York.

Khan, Almaz 1995. "Chinggis Khan: From Imperial Ancestor to Ethnic Hero," in *Cultural Encounters on China's Ethnic Frontiers*, ed. S. Harrel. 248–277. Seattle & London.

Khazanov, Anatoly M. 2003. "A State Without a Nation? Russia after Empire," in *The Nation State in Question*, ed. T. V. Paul *et al.* 79–105. Princeton.

Langlois, John, ed. 1981. *China under Mongol Rule.* Princeton.

Liu Xiaoyuan 1999. "The Kuomingtang and the 'Mongolian Question' in the Chinese Civil War, 1945–1949," *Inner Asia* 1: 169–194.

Mao Tse-tung (Mao Zedong) 1959. *Poems.* Beijing.

Okada, H. 1998. "China as a Successor State to the Mongol Empire," in *The Mongol Empire and its Legacy.* Eds. D. O. Morgan and R. Amitai-Preiss. 260–272. Leiden.

Ostrowski, Donald 1998. *Muscovy and the Mongols*. Cambridge.

Perdue, Peter 2005. *China Marches West:The Qing Conquest of Central Eurasia*. Cambridge MA.

Phillips, J. R. S. 1998. *The Medieval Expansion of Europe*. 2nd edition. Oxford.

Qiu Shushen 2002. "LunYuan dai Zhongguo shaoshu minzu xin tanju ji qi shehui yingxiang," (On the New Pattern of National Minorities and its Impact on theYuan Society [sic]), in *Abstracts of Papers Given in the International Conference on Mongol-Yuan Studies*. 143. Nanjing.

Rossabi, Morris 1988. *Khubilai Khan*. Berkeley.

Smith, P. J. and R. von Glann, eds. 2003. *The Song-Yuan-Ming Transition in Chinese History*. Cambridge MA.

Sabloff, Paula 2002. "Why Mongolia?The Political Culture of an Emerging Democracy," *Central Asian Survey*, 21: 19–36.

Skrynnikova,Tatiana 2005. "ObrazTsingiskhana v sovremennom Buriatskom istoriko kulturnom diskurse [The Image of Chinggis Khan in Contemporary Buriat Historical and Cultural Discourse]." *Ab Imperio* 6/4. (*http://abimperio.net/scgi-bin/aishow.pl?state = showa&idart = 1455&idling = 2&Code =* accessed 18 May 2006).

Stewart, Kevin 1997. *The Mongols inWestern/American Consciousness*. Lewiston, NewYork.

Trubetzkoy, Nicolai S. 1991. "The Legacy of Genghis Khan:A Perspective on Russian History not from theWest but from the East (1925)" in his collected volume *The Legacy of Genghis Khan*, ed.A. Lieberman. 161–232. Ann Arbor: Michigan Slavic Publications.

Watson, Geoff 2002. "Western Images of Central Asia c. 1200–1800," in *The Turks*, eds. H.C. Güzel, C.Cem Oghuz and O. Karatay.Vol. 2: 795–804. Ankara.

Zerjal,Tatiana et al, 2003. "The Genetic Legacy of the Mongols," *American Journal of Human Genetics*, 72: 717–721.

INDEX

(Arrangement of subheadings is alphabetical, except under Chinggis Khan, **life** and **military career**, where they are arranged in page number order)

Merv 86
military institutions 106
military intelligence 56, 71
military knowledge 72
Ming dynasty 82, 106, 146
Mirkhwand 109
mobilization of people 85–6, 89
Moghul dynasty 83, 104
Moghulistan 82, 83, 84, 99
Möngke (Chinggis's grandson) 78–80,
  86, 98, 122
Mongol empire 76, 80; administration of
  66–7, 76, 78; divided into khanates
  80–1, 99; geopolitical changes
  99–102; globalizing effect 85–93;
  languages of 66, 75, 93; legacy of
  imperial culture 75; restoration of
  damage 65, 67
Mongolia 7, 80, 81, 82, 88; Buddhism in
  81, 139–40, 141, 142; Chinese
  colonization of 141–2; image of
  Chinggis in 138–45; independent
  143–4; Inner 7, 142, 149, 150;
  institutional changes 41–6; Islam in
  94; literary renaissance 139–40;
  nationalism in 142–3, 160; nomadic
  empires 11–12, 14–15; Outer 7,
  140, 142, 149, 151; population of
  85; re-organization of army 41–2;
  reorganized by Chinggis 41–6; in
  Russian civil war 142; as Soviet
  satellite 142–3; supremacy of
  Chinggis 38, 39; tribes in 9–11,
  28–32
Mongols 6–7, 29–32; Americans
  compared with 131; Arab
  nationalism and 129–30, 131;
  cruelty of 63, 64–5; diet of 120;
  islamization of 161–2; legacy from
  predecessors 22–3; loyalty to
  Chinggis 38; origin myths 29, 31,
  114–15; predecessors 14–23; and
  Qara Khitai 18
monotheization of Chinggis 111, 112–21

Montesquieu, Charles de 157
Morgan, D. 43, 68
Moscow 84, 99
Muhammad, the Prophet 109, 110, 121
Muhammad Khwarazm Shah 22, 25,
  54–5; Chinggis and 54–5, 56; defeat
  of 58–9
Munis, Muhammad 125–6
Muqali (general) 42, 52
Muscovy 84, 101, 102; Chinggisid
  principle in 102–4
Muslim literature, depictions of
  Chinggis in 109–136; as enemy of
  Islam 109, 111, 114, 129; as
  legitimator of political order 124–8;
  as monotheist 112–21; origin myths
  114–18, 140; universal histories
  109, 127
Muslim world: arts in 90, 91; Chinggis's
  conquests in 53–61, 62, 63–9;
  image of Chinggis in 160–2;
  knowledge in 89–90; religious life,
  post-conquest 67–8; Turks in
  18–21

Naimans 17, 28–9, 36, 42, 102; coalition
  with Merkids 39, 45–6; defeat of
  38–9
Najm al-Din Ghazi 112
al-Nasir, Caliph (1185–1225) 22
nationalism 3, 129–32, 142, 148, 151,
  153, 154, 160, 162
Nishapur 60
Nogais 84, 101
nökers (companions) 10; of Chinggis 35,
  41, 42
nomadic empires 11–12; relations with
  sedentary states 11, 14, 26, 62,
  64–5
nomadism 7–12, 102
Nurgachi 147
al-Nuwayri, Shihab al-Din 119–20

Oghuz Khan 115, 116, 134